*Teen Love*®
# ON RELATIONSHIPS

*Teen Love* ® *Series*

# ON RELATIONSHIPS

*A Book for Teenagers*

## KIMBERLY KIRBERGER

Chicken Soup for the Teenage Soul *series*

**HCI TEENS**

**Health Communications, Inc.**
**Deerfield Beach, Florida**

*www.hci-online.com*
*www.love4teens.com*

We would like to acknowledge the many publishers and individuals who granted us permission to reprint the cited material. (Note: The stories that were penned anonymously, that are in the public domain or that were written by Kimberly Kirberger are not included in this listing.)

*Falling in Love.* Reprinted by permission of Kent Nerburn. Excerpted from *Letters to My Son* by Kent Nerburn. ©1996 Kent Nerburn.

*My Best Feature.* Reprinted by permission of Sara Nachtman. ©1999 Sara Nachtman.

*I Am Enough.* Reprinted by permission of Chelsea Hellings. ©1999 Chelsea Hellings.

*Loving Without Limits.* Reprinted by permission of Kelly Garnett. ©1999 Kelly Garnett.

*I Wonder.* Reprinted by permission of Miriam Perez. ©1999 Miriam Perez.

*Dreaming of Me.* Reprinted by permission of Miriam Perez. ©1999 Miriam Perez.

*(continued on page 369)*

**Library of Congress Cataloging-in-Publication Data**

Kirberger, Kimberly, date.
    Teen love: on relationships: a book for teenagers / Kimberly Kirberger.
        p. cm.
    Summary: Combines personal advice with poetry and stories about teenage love and relationships.
    ISBN 1-55874-734-6
    1. Teenagers Life skills guides Juvenile literature. 2. Man-woman relationships Juvenile literature. 3. Interpersonal relations Juvenile literature. 4. Love Juvenile literature.
    [1. Interpersonal relationships. 2. Love.]
    HQ796.K477 1999
    306.7'0835—dc21                                                    99-38645
                                                                       CIP

Publisher: Health Communications, Inc.
          3201 S.W. 15th Street
          Deerfield Beach, FL 33442-8190

R-01-01

*Cover and inside book design by Lawna Patterson Oldfield*

*With love I dedicate this book:*

*To my mother, who is my dearest friend and who taught me many things about love.*

*To my father, who always made me feel like I was the most beautiful girl in the world.*

*To my son, Jesse. May your love life bring you much happiness and joy.*

*And to my husband, John, the love of my life.*

# Contents

Acknowledgments . . . . . . . . . . . . . . . . . . . . . . . . . . . . . .xv
Love 1A: Introduction . . . . . . . . . . . . . . . . . . . . . . . . . .xix
Guidelines for Reading This Book . . . . . . . . . . . . . . . .xxi
Falling in Love  *Kent Nerburn* . . . . . . . . . . . . . . . . . . .xxv

## 1. First and Foremost:
## You Gotta Love Yourself!

Love Yourself First . . . . . . . . . . . . . . . . . . . . . . . . . . . . .2
My Best Feature  *Sara Nachtman* . . . . . . . . . . . . . . . . . .5
Is There Someone Out There for Me? . . . . . . . . . . . . . . .7
I Am Enough  *Chelsea Hellings* . . . . . . . . . . . . . . . . . . .9
Loving Without Limits  *Kelly Garnett* . . . . . . . . . . . . .11
Everyone Has a Boyfriend but Me . . . . . . . . . . . . . . . . .14
I Wonder  *Miriam Perez* . . . . . . . . . . . . . . . . . . . . . . .16
Why Do All the Girls Like Older Guys Now? . . . . . . . .17
Am I Good Enough for Him? . . . . . . . . . . . . . . . . . . . .20
I'm Losing My Confidence . . . . . . . . . . . . . . . . . . . . . .24
I'm Not Pretty Enough for Him . . . . . . . . . . . . . . . . . .26
Dreaming of Me  *Miriam Perez* . . . . . . . . . . . . . . . . . .28

## 2. Falling in Love

Falling in Love . . . . . . . . . . . . . . . . . . . . . . . . . . . . . .30

The Perfect Guy? *Katie Brennan* . . . . . . . . . . . . . . . . .31

Is This Love? . . . . . . . . . . . . . . . . . . . . . . . . . . . . . . . . .35

You Tell Me *Kim Llerena* . . . . . . . . . . . . . . . . . . . . . .38

I Can't Open Up . . . and Now I've Lost Him . . . . . . . .41

Stone by Stone *Rachel Bentley* . . . . . . . . . . . . . . . . .44

I'm in Love with Love! . . . . . . . . . . . . . . . . . . . . . . . . .47

She's Been Hurt, and Now She Won't Love . . . . . . . . .49

The Pit of Love *Jennifer Hadra* . . . . . . . . . . . . . . . . .51

My Special Someone *Kristine Lee* . . . . . . . . . . . . . . .53

Help . . . I'm Afraid of Falling! . . . . . . . . . . . . . . . . . . .56

## 3. All These New Feelings

All These New Feelings . . . . . . . . . . . . . . . . . . . . . . . . .60

The "L" Word *Amanda Bailey* . . . . . . . . . . . . . . . . . . .65

What Is He Thinking? . . . . . . . . . . . . . . . . . . . . . . . . . .68

My Friend Stole My Crush . . . . . . . . . . . . . . . . . . . . . .70

Sister *Becca Woolf* . . . . . . . . . . . . . . . . . . . . . . . . . . . .72

I Have to Choose Between Two Guys . . . . . . . . . . . . . .75

I'm Unlucky in Love . . . . . . . . . . . . . . . . . . . . . . . . . . .77

Oh, No . . . She Wants to Have a "Talk"! . . . . . . . . . . . .80

This Guy Is Spreading Rumors About Me . . . . . . . . . .83

Alone *Becca Woolf* . . . . . . . . . . . . . . . . . . . . . . . . . . . .85

I'm a Sensitive Guy . . . . . . . . . . . . . . . . . . . . . . . . . . . .86

## 4. There Is a First Time for Everything: Love Is the Part of Us That Is Real

A First Time for Everything ...................... .90

First Time  *Jane Watkins* ........................ .92

I'm Afraid She'll Reject Me ...  .................. .93

I Misjudged a Great Guy  ........................ .96

I'm Scared to Kiss Him ........................... .98

I'm Graduating from High School ...
    and I've Never Even Been Kissed .............. .100

First Kiss  *Ron Cheng*  ........................ .103

The Kiss  *Allison Forster*  .................... .106

I'm Nervous to Make the First Move  ............ .108

I Don't Get It: What Is Love?  .................. .110

Love Is Sweet  *Tiffany Storm*  ................ .113

## 5. Do You Like Me???

Do You Like Me? ................................. .117

The Boy Next Door  *Becca Woolf* ............... .119

What Do Guys Like? What Do Girls Like? ......... .123

Illusion  *Julian Arizona* ..................... .127

I Freeze When I'm Around Her ................... .130

How Can I Tell If He Likes Me? ................. .133

How Can I Tell If She Likes Me?  ............... .136

We Make Out ... and Then It's Over ............. .138

Sweet Dreams  *Kelly Garnett* .................. .140

Someone Special  *Olivia Odom*  ................ .143

## 6. When Friends Become More . . .

When Friends Become More . . .  . . . . . . . . . . . . . . . .146

My Best Friend  *Samantha Joseph*  . . . . . . . . . . . . . .148

Help . . . I Have a Raging Crush on My Best Friend! . .152

The Key to My Heart  *Tammy Osborne*  . . . . . . . . . . .156

The Day We Became More . . .  *Brandy Nicholas* . . . . .157

I've Fallen for My Friend  . . . . . . . . . . . . . . . . . . . . . .159

With Honor  *Erin Kelly*  . . . . . . . . . . . . . . . . . . . . . .162

I Want Him to Be My Boyfriend . . . Not Just
    a Friend . . . . . . . . . . . . . . . . . . . . . . . . . . . . . . . . .163

More Than Friends  *Anonymous*  . . . . . . . . . . . . . . . .166

I Finally Got the Girl—Now What Do I Do?  . . . . . . . .169

Are We Better Off Just Being Friends?  . . . . . . . . . . .172

My Friend Talked to My Crush and Ruined
    Everything  . . . . . . . . . . . . . . . . . . . . . . . . . . . . . .174

Good-Bye  *Becca Woolf*  . . . . . . . . . . . . . . . . . . . . . .177

I Like Her . . . but She Likes My Friend . . . . . . . . . . .178

Identical Friends  *Jane Watkins*  . . . . . . . . . . . . . . .181

## 7. Unrequited Love

Unrequited Love . . . . . . . . . . . . . . . . . . . . . . . . . . . . .184

Stupid Horse Jokes  *Briana Halpin*  . . . . . . . . . . . . .187

The Letter I'll Never Send  *Rebecca Scida* . . . . . . . . .190

He Doesn't Know I Exist . . . . . . . . . . . . . . . . . . . . . . .192

I Can't Forget Him  . . . . . . . . . . . . . . . . . . . . . . . . . . .194

I'm Obsessing Big Time  . . . . . . . . . . . . . . . . . . . . . . .196

No Matter What I Do, She'll Never Like Me Back . . . .198

He Doesn't Love Me Back . . . . . . . . . . . . . . . . . . . . . .200

All I Can't Say  *Nina Yocco* . . . . . . . . . . . . . . . . . . . .202

I'm Waiting for Her to Decide . . . . . . . . . . . . . . . . . . .204

Help . . . I'm Obsessing Over My Crush! . . . . . . . . . . . .206

She Loves Someone Else . . . . . . . . . . . . . . . . . . . . . . .210

I'm Obsessing Over Him . . . . . . . . . . . . . . . . . . . . . . .212

## 8. Now That We're Together

Now That We're Together . . . . . . . . . . . . . . . . . . . . . . .216

Those Three Words!  *Amy Ortega* . . . . . . . . . . . . . . . .219

One Minute She's Nice, the Next She's Mean:

   What Am I Doing Wrong? . . . . . . . . . . . . . . . . . . . . .220

My Boyfriend Treats Me Badly Around His Friends . .225

My Boyfriend Loves Me More Than I Love Him . . . . .228

How Do I Save Our Relationship? . . . . . . . . . . . . . . . .230

We Are So Different . . . . . . . . . . . . . . . . . . . . . . . . . .234

I'm Tired of Being Compared to Other Guys . . . . . . .237

We Just Had a Fight, and My Boyfriend Snapped . . . .240

I'm Finally Happy. . . . Can It Last? . . . . . . . . . . . . . . .243

Shadows Dance  *Becca Woolf* . . . . . . . . . . . . . . . . . . .246

I Don't Trust My Boyfriend . . . . . . . . . . . . . . . . . . . . .249

I'm Always Worried He'll Find Someone Better . . . . . .252

Fear  *Meredee Switzer* . . . . . . . . . . . . . . . . . . . . . . .254

The Love of My Life Moved Away . . . . . . . . . . . . . . . .257

My Parents Don't Approve of My Boyfriend . . . . . . . .259

My Boyfriend Ignored Me at a Party . . . . . . . . . . . . . .263

My Boyfriend Pays More Attention to
  My Parents Than to Me! . . . . . . . . . . . . . . . . . . . . .267

Can Our Cyber-Love Be for Real? . . . . . . . . . . . . . . . .270

My Virtual Relationship Is Real to Me . . . . . . . . . . . .275

## 9. Breaking Up Is Hard to Do

Breaking Up Is Hard to Do . . . . . . . . . . . . . . . . . . . . . .278

For Zack  *Brandy Nicholas* . . . . . . . . . . . . . . . . . .280

My First Heartbreak  *Anonymous* . . . . . . . . . . . . . .282

Untrue Love  *Sara Corbin* . . . . . . . . . . . . . . . . . . . .285

I Really Blew It, and Now I've Lost Him . . . . . . . . . .288

Reunited: A Two-Sided Poem  *Becca Woolf* . . . . . . . .291

She's Moved On, and I Can't Handle It . . . . . . . . . . .293

It Hurts So Much to Have Lost Him . . . . . . . . . . . . .296

Love Lessons  *Kelly Garnett* . . . . . . . . . . . . . . . . . . .299

It's So Hard  *Becca Woolf* . . . . . . . . . . . . . . . . . . . . .302

I Couldn't Wait for Her to Decide . . . . . . . . . . . . . . .304

Dried-Out Roses  *Becca Woolf* . . . . . . . . . . . . . . . . .306

How Do I Break Up with My Boyfriend? . . . . . . . . . .307

Breaking Up Is Hard to Do  *Lynnsey Gardner* . . . . . .311

Speechless  *Kira Bindrim* . . . . . . . . . . . . . . . . . . . . .316

We Broke Up, and I'm So Depressed . . . . . . . . . . . . .317

Lost  *Becca Woolf* . . . . . . . . . . . . . . . . . . . . . . . . . . .319

Where's My Heart?: A Ballad  *Becca Woolf* . . . . . . . .320

I Ignored My Friends for Love . . . and Now I
   Want Them Back . . . . . . . . . . . . . . . . . . . . . . . . . .322
At First  *Becca Woolf* . . . . . . . . . . . . . . . . . . . . . . .324
Adios  *Langley Wetzel* . . . . . . . . . . . . . . . . . . . . . . .326

## 10. Starting Over . . . or Here We Go Again

Starting Over . . . . . . . . . . . . . . . . . . . . . . . . . . . . .330
I'm Having a Hard Time Letting Go . . . . . . . . . . . . . .332
To Let Go  *Tiffany Appleton* . . . . . . . . . . . . . . . . . . .334
A New Start  *Becca Woolf* . . . . . . . . . . . . . . . . . . . .336
My Private Pain  *Anonymous* . . . . . . . . . . . . . . . . . .337
What If I Get Hurt Again? . . . . . . . . . . . . . . . . . . . . .341
Chasm of the Heart  *Rachel Miller* . . . . . . . . . . . . . .343
Footprints in My Heart  *Lauren Olszewski* . . . . . . . .344
I Just Moved, and It's Hard to Start Over . . . . . . . . . .347
I'm Having Fun on My Own! . . . . . . . . . . . . . . . . . . .350
Who Needs a Boyfriend Anyway?  *Shelby Woodard* . . .352
I'm Becoming Obsessed Again! . . . . . . . . . . . . . . . . . .354

In Closing . . . . . . . . . . . . . . . . . . . . . . . . . . . . . . . .359
Who Is Kimberly Kirberger? . . . . . . . . . . . . . . . . . . .360
Contributors . . . . . . . . . . . . . . . . . . . . . . . . . . . . . .362
Permissions *(continued)* . . . . . . . . . . . . . . . . . . . . . .369

# Acknowledgments

It is always an honor when we have the chance to thank people who help us. We all have practiced our fantasy acceptance speech for the Academy Awards or dreamed about having an opportunity to adequately acknowledge those who have blessed our lives. With this kind of excitement and gratitude, I acknowledge the following people:

To Jack Canfield, my brother and my friend, for giving me the opportunity of a lifetime, for believing in me and for continuing to love and support me in the most essential ways. Jack, you are my hero!

To my husband, John, who is the smartest, funniest and sweetest person in the whole world. I love you totally, John.

To my son, Jesse, who inspires me on a daily basis and who taught me a whole new definition of love. Jesse, you are the best!

To my parents, Ellen Taylor and Fred Angelis, for putting up with me through all my loves and heartbreaks. Trust me, this was no small feat. I love you both with all my heart.

To Patty Hansen and Mark Victor Hansen, for welcoming me into the *Chicken Soup* family, for giving me the amazing opportunities you have, and for being such an inspiration to me, in many ways.

To Peter Vegso, for believing in me, supporting me and making what would normally be "work" into something more valuable and definitely more fun.

To Mitch Claspy, for the countless things he does for me and for I.A.M. for Teens, for being such a pleasure to work with and for being who he is.

To Tasha Boucher, for helping me with literally each and every aspect of this book. I could not have done it without her. All the fun we had was just a bonus!

To Becca Woolf, for her wonderful feedback, her incredible poetry and for being such an inspirational teenager.

To Lia Gay, for showing me how lovable teenagers can be and for all her help on this book. You will always be the daughter I wished I had. I love you, Lia.

To Nina Palais, for running the Teen Letter Project with such love, and for all the other things she does to help my life run smoothly.

To Paula De Leon, for handling so many things, from permissions to travel arrangements. Paula, Mitch and I appreciate you more than you will ever know.

To Myra Raney, for all her hard work and for inspiring me with her personal metamorphosis and her very sweet soul.

To all the teens who are part of the Teen Letter Project: Arianna Axelrod, Nicole Berger, Esme Ganz, Dawn Geer, Blake Harrington, Lael Humphries, Rose Lannutti, Jamie Lauren, Aleph Orozco, Azia Patrick,

Jesse Petersen, Ashley Sawtelle and Rachael Schaefer.

To Jessie Braun, for her loyalty, support and friendship, and for always having the perfect insights.

To Lisa Gumenick, Lisa Rothbard, Lindsey Ross, Bree Abel and Hana Ivanhoe, for being such excellent examples of what teenagers can be if given love and respect. Most of all, thank you for your feedback and support. You guys, I love you—you have taught me so much.

To Ashley, Haley, Caitlin, Hanah, Lilly, Sarah, Derek, Morgan, Blake and Tommy, it's so great to have you guys in my life.

To my dearest friends: Kim Foley, Inga Mahoney, Barbara De Angelis, Mary Ellen Klee, Lynar Abel, Steve, Claudia, David and Bava Stroud, your friendship means the world to me. Thanks for your love.

To Patty Aubery, Heather McNamara and Nancy Mitchell, for their love and support.

To Matthew Diener, for being such an excellent editor, answering my endless questions and always being so patient.

To Lisa Drucker, for being such a pleasure to work with, while doing such a great job. Thanks for making me feel special.

To Kim Weiss and Larry Getlen, for their brilliant and amazing public relations efforts.

To Lawna Oldfield, for her work on the cover and for typesetting the manuscript.

To Terry Burke, for his awesome sales work and for keeping us all laughing.

To Lori Golden, Irena Xanthos and Jane Barone, for believing in this project and being so supportive.

To Kelly Maragni, Randee Feldman and Yvonne zum Tobel for their brilliant marketing work.

To Karen Ornstein, Doreen Hess and Lisa Baxter and their staff, for doing all they do to make the customers of Health Communications happy.

I am truly grateful for the many hands and hearts that made this book possible. I love you all.

# Love 1A: Introduction

---

♥

---

Till it has loved, no man
or woman can become itself.

Emily Dickinson

---

If you are reading this book you have probably already been stung by the love bug. A boy or girl in your class or youth group suddenly made your heart beat a little faster, and you finally understood this love thing that everyone had been talking about.

First let me give you a warm welcome into the world of love and relationships. As with life, it isn't all fun and games, but the more you know, the better you will be at handling what comes your way. Much of what you need to know can only be taught by the great teacher: experience.

In this book, some have shared that experience. Some have shared it through poetry, some through stories and some with commonly asked questions. I have done my best to answer these questions without giving that all-too-annoying thing: adult advice. I do hope I have been able to share some of my wisdom, to show my compassion, and, most of all, to help you see that when it comes to love, it is much simpler than we choose to make it. Nothing is more wonderful than sharing love with another person; it is just that we tend to complicate, confuse and distort it.

Love is a wonderful thing. When your heart opens up and you see another person through loving eyes, it is truly one of life's best experiences. When another person looks at you in that special way, you will think you have discovered heaven on earth.

The advice and wisdom that I share with you in this book is so you can enjoy love when it's happening and let it go when it is not. It is to help you to keep it simple, keep it honest, and, most of all, keep it fun. My hope for you is that you can enjoy the journey and learn as you go. Every relationship that you have is an opportunity to learn and grow.

The most important thing I can do is help you to not take it all too personally. Love can have its own reasons for things that we know nothing about at the time they are happening. Maybe one relationship wasn't meant to work out so that when another one came along you would be available.

We never know. Unfortunately, we often blame ourselves when love doesn't work. We think if someone doesn't love us or want to be with us, then there must be something wrong with us, and this just isn't true.

Love is a great teacher; I think it is the best. Learning is often painful. Just remember: You will never lose at love if you always ask it what it is teaching you, and you listen very carefully when it answers.

Enjoy the journey. . . .

# Guidelines for Reading This Book

♥

We read books to find out
who we are. What other people,
real or imaginary, do and think and
feel is an essential guide to our
understanding of what we ourselves
are and may become.

Ursula K. Le Guin

I have divided this book into ten different chapters.
This was challenging in itself because so many things in
love aren't that simple. In fact, I became aware of what
I now believe to be the biggest problem in the area of
love. It is very disorganized. If we were able to put our
life and our relationships into neat little compartments,
we wouldn't have half the problems or heartache that
we have now.

Take, for example, the chapter "There Is a First Time
for Everything." This seemed simple enough . . . first

crush, first love, first relationship, etc. I went through the pile of letters I had designated for this chapter and began reading: "When I was with Ben I thought I was in love. However, now that I am with Ryan I see what my mom was saying. I had no idea what love was." Then I had to decide: Does this go into the chapter called "All These New Feelings" or should I keep it in "There Is a First Time for Everything"?

Then I moved on to the chapter on "When Friends Become More . . ." If I only had to deal with simple things like "I fell in love with my best friend," it would have been a piece of cake. The following is an example of the kinds of questions I did find for this chapter: "I hated this guy. He was such a creep, but my friend Sarah liked him and begged me to give him another chance, as a friend. So I did. The next thing I knew he liked me, but I mean he LIKED me liked me and Sarah wasn't too happy about this. Brad and I ended up being together but it didn't last very long. I fell in love with his friend, Sam. Sarah was happy, so we were friends again and after a while Brad and I were best friends, too. We spent hours on the phone talking about Sarah and Sam. My question is this, I am starting to like Brad again and if I tell anyone I will lose two friends and a boyfriend. Please tell me what to do."

So, as you can see, my job of dividing these questions into chapters wasn't easy but I did my best. While reading this book, please remember: There may be friendship issues in the "All These New Feelings" chapter and there will be breakup issues in the "Starting Over" chapter.

I recommend that you read through the whole book once. Then, when you have a specific problem that you need help with, turn to the chapter that best represents your situation. If you want more information than what you find in that chapter, skip around to other relevant chapters.

This book is filled with questions and answers, great poetry and stories that illustrate the experience of love. The questions and the answers are all written by me. I have read over a thousand questions submitted to our Web-page forums* and interviewed hundreds of teens about their experiences with love. From all this reading and talking with teens, I have been able to get an idea of the important questions and concerns that teens are dealing with today. I have written the questions myself in order to keep personal information private, to make the questions clear and concise, and to make sure that the personal details of somebody's situation don't get in the way of everyone's ability to relate to the issue being discussed. Many of you will recognize bits and pieces of your questions but will be able to avoid what could possibly be an embarrassing situation because I've changed personal details such as names.

I am extremely excited about the quality of the poetry in the book. Good poems, like those written for this book, express the feelings associated with being in love so precisely that many people will feel that the poems were

---

* The *Chicken Soup for the Teenage Soul* Web page. The Web-page address is: *www.teenagechickensoup.com.*

written especially for them. All the different feelings that arise when one is in love are hard to define. They can be even harder to express to another person. I hope you can read the poetry in this book and have the experience of "Yes, that is what I am feeling!" and know without a doubt that you are not alone. You can also use the poems to show your friends or your significant other how you feel.

Last, but not least, we have included some stories. All of them were written by teens (except two that I wrote), and all of them are about love and the lessons love teaches us.

This is a book that was written entirely for you. It is all about love and relationships, and it is packed full of compassion, concern and wisdom. I hope that as you read each page you feel that it was written specifically for you. I hope you feel that your questions are being answered and your feelings are being expressed. Most of all, I hope that—no matter what you are going through—this book helps you, guides you and shows you that you are not alone. If I have achieved these three things, then I have succeeded.

Please let me know.

I can be reached at:

Kimberly Kirberger
P.O. Box 936
Pacific Palisades, CA 90272

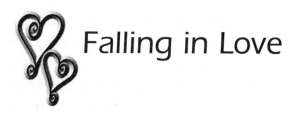 # Falling in Love

*Kent Nerburn*

Love is life. . . .
And if you miss love, you miss life.

Leo Buscaglia

It is a mystery why we fall in love.

It is a mystery how it happens. It is a mystery when it comes. It is a mystery why some loves grow and it is a mystery why some loves fail.

You can analyze this mystery and look for reasons and causes, but you will never do any more than take the life out of the experience. Just as life itself is something more than the sum of the bones and muscles and electrical impulses in the body, love is something more than the sum of the interests and attractions and commonalities that two people share. And just as life itself is a gift that comes and goes in its own time, so, too, the coming of love must be taken as an unfathomable gift that cannot be questioned in its ways.

Sometimes—hopefully at least once in your life—the gift of love will come to you in full flower, and you will take hold of it and celebrate it in all its inexpressible beauty. This is the dream we all share. More often, it will come and take hold of you, celebrate you for a brief moment, then move on.

When this happens to young people, they too often try to grasp the love and hold it to them, refusing to see that it is a gift freely given and a gift that just as freely moves away. When they fall out of love or the person they love feels the spirit of love leaving, they try desperately to reclaim the love that is lost rather than accepting the gift for what it was, then moving on.

They want answers where there are no answers. They want to know what is wrong with them that makes the other person no longer love them, or they try to get their lover to change, thinking that if some small thing were different love would bloom again. They blame their circumstances and say that if they go far away and start a new life together their love will grow.

They try anything to give meaning to what has happened. But there is no meaning beyond the love itself, and until they accept its own mysterious ways they live in a sea of misery.

You need to know this about love, and to accept it. You need to treat what it brings you with kindness. If you find yourself in love with a person who does not love you, be gentle with yourself. There is nothing wrong with you. Love just didn't choose to rest in the other person's heart.

If you find someone else in love with you and you don't love him or her, feel honored that love came and called at your door, but gently refuse the gift you cannot return. Do not take advantage, do not cause pain. How you deal with love is how love will deal with you, and all our hearts feel the same pains and joys, even if our lives and ways are very different.

If you fall in love with another and she falls in love with you, and then love chooses to leave, do not try to reclaim it or assess blame. Let it go. There is a reason and there is a meaning. You will know in time, but time itself will choose the moment.

Remember that you don't choose love. Love chooses you.

All you can really do is accept it for all its mystery when it comes into your life. Feel the way it fills you to overflowing, then reach out and give it away. Give it back to the person who brought it alive in you. Give it to others who seem poor in spirit. Give it to the world around you in any way you can.

This is where so many lovers go wrong. Having been so long without love, they understand love only as a need. They see their hearts as empty places that will be filled by love, and they begin to look at love as something that flows to them rather than from them.

In the first blush of new love they are filled to overflowing, but as their love cools they revert to seeing their love as a need. They cease to be someone who generates love and instead become someone who seeks love. They forget that the secret of love is that it is a gift, and that it can be made to grow only by giving it away.

Remember this and keep it in your heart. Love has its own time, its own season, and its own reasons for coming and going. You cannot bribe it or coerce it or reason it into staying. You can only embrace it when it arrives and give it away when it comes to you. But if it chooses to leave, from your heart or from the heart of your lover, there is nothing you can do and nothing you should do. Love has always been and will always be a mystery. Be glad that it came to live for a moment in your life. If you keep your heart open, it will come again.

*One*

# First and Foremost: You Gotta Love Yourself!

*Each relationship you have
with another person reflects the
relationship you have
with yourself.*

Alice Deville

# *Love Yourself First*

♥

## To love oneself is the beginning of a life-long romance.

Oscar Wilde

Before we get started with relationships, let's take a look at the most important relationship we will ever have. . . . the one with ourselves.

When asked if they like/love themselves, most people would respond with a quick *yes*. However, were they to examine their feelings further, these people would come to the same conclusion that I have. I am my own worst enemy. I would not tolerate anyone treating me the way I treat myself. I would leave the room or hang up the phone if anyone dared to say the things to me that I say to myself. I second-guess myself, lecture myself, judge myself and sometimes even punish myself. As for compassion, I tend to save that for my friends. At least that's how it used to be. My approach to myself is improving because I have consciously started to change it.

The first step to changing anything is to be aware of it. We must be honest about how we treat ourselves.

For example:

How do you talk to yourself?
Are you confident?
Do you speak kindly to yourself?
Are you secure and peaceful in most situations?
Do you like the way you look, act, are?

If you are like most of us, you think you could lose some weight, have better skin, have a more exciting life and a smaller nose. We pick at ourselves. We think that everyone else is happy with the way he or she is. We think that security is something other people have, and we are the ones who missed out. Here's a little secret. Everybody is insecure. Everybody judges himself or herself harshly, and everybody struggles with even the *concept* of loving himself or herself.

The good news is that once we become aware of the way we treat ourselves, we can change it. The most worthwhile goal you can ever set for yourself is one of self-love and self-acceptance. Once we begin to strive for self-acceptance, once we realize that we are supposed to accept ourselves, our lives will begin to change before our very eyes.

Let's start by looking at some of the obstacles we put in the way of self-acceptance. First, we think love is something that has to be earned. We look at ourselves and say, "I will love myself when I am thinner. I will love myself when I stop messing up so much. I will love myself when I stop being so insecure. I will accept myself when I can be like so-and-so, or I will accept myself when I am no longer the way I am."

We all engage in this kind of thinking, but do you see how silly and absurd it is?

What if I told you that the more you love yourself the more lovable you will be?

The best possible person that you can be . . . can only be when you love yourself completely.

Would you say to your best friend, "I can't love you until you lose weight"?

Would you say, "I don't love you because you aren't perfect. You keep messing up"?

Of course you wouldn't. And yet this is how we speak to ourselves.

Have you ever had the experience of being nice to someone who was feeling down? Have you ever complimented someone and then seen that person transform right before your eyes? He or she instantly becomes more attractive or funnier. You say something nice to someone and his or her face glows and his or her eyes get a little sparkle. This isn't your imagination. This is true transformation. The very same thing will happen to you when you compliment yourself. Try it. . . .

My heart is with you as you begin to work on accepting yourself. Remember that loving yourself can open the door to a whole new life, one that has as part of it relationships of the very best kind.

# My Best Feature

SARA NACHTMAN

I asked my friend this afternoon,
As I gazed into my reflection,
What she thought of what I saw.
She said, "Images are usually misconceptions."

I started to put down my appearance,
Wishing I was thinner or taller.
She looked at me with understanding eyes,
Saying, "Superficial wishes only make you smaller."

I knew she was right, but who was she to talk,
For she was every guy's dream.
I tried to point this out to her,
She replied, "Appearances aren't always what they seem."

"Tell me five features you admire in yourself," she said,
And I knew my troubles had just begun,
For I could see the hurt in her expression,
When I couldn't even think of one.

I could not think of a single feature I liked,
And I could feel my stomach slowly start to sink.
So I turned to my friend and simply said,
"Well what do you think?"

"I think you're looking at it all wrong," she said
"And I wish I could make it clearer.
It's what's inside you that makes you beautiful,
And not what can be seen in the mirror."

She said, "You're the most loving person I know,
And I hate to watch you fall apart.
If you want to know what makes you beautiful to me,
Your best feature is your heart."

# Is There Someone Out There for Me?

♥

## A person's looks are never going to make you love them or like them.

Drew Barrymore

*Dear Kim,*

*I am feeling really depressed lately. All my friends have boyfriends and I have never had one. Honestly, I don't think any guy will ever like me. I am a little overweight and not what you would call a beauty. The sad thing is, I would really like to have a boyfriend. I am too embarrassed to talk to my friends about guys because I am afraid they will just feel sorry for me. What should I do?*

You know, the great thing about love is that there is someone for everyone. I think there are two important things for you to think about.

The first is loving yourself. I know it sounds like something that people just say, but people who love themselves are very attractive to other people.

The second is: Not all people judge others by their looks. If you take good care of yourself—exercise and eat well and feel good about yourself, just as you are—I promise there are guys who will be interested in you.

Sometimes, things don't happen when we want them to, but sooner or later you will have a boyfriend (and a new set of problems). Don't worry: Everyone finds love. Those who have to wait a little longer just appreciate it more when it comes.

# I Am Enough

CHELSEA HELLINGS

"You cannot change what is a part of you,"
although I've often tried.
My body was never thin enough,
my imperfections I'd always hide.

I smiled when they said I was beautiful,
I laughed when they said I was great.
But it took a long time to believe in their words,
I figured loneliness was my fate.

The boys I wanted didn't want me,
I was tossed, used and torn.
So many took me as a joke,
I crawled inside myself—scared and forlorn.

My self-esteem had let me down,
my belief in myself was nil.
I did not understand where I was headed,
Could not understand until. . . .

I finally decided to believe in me,
I realized that I was worth so much.
This was when I could see through the storm,
when I allowed my soul to be touched.

I sometimes wish for money and love,
when times get distressing and tough.
But I know that I will always love myself,
no matter what—
I AM ENOUGH!

# Loving Without Limits

KELLY GARNETT

I don't believe makeup and
the right hairstyle alone can make a
woman beautiful. The most radiant
woman in the room is the one full
of life and experience.

Sharon Stone

I just didn't understand why he had agreed to go out
with me. . . . I mean, he was absolutely gorgeous, the
kind of guy you see and try not to get caught staring at.
But I had been caught. And for some reason completely
unknown to me, he not only smiled back, but he called
me. He asked me out. And there I was, two blocks away
from our first date, wishing I had worn the gray shirt
instead of the blue one.

It took me over an hour to finally relax, but when I
did, I began to realize that not only was he good-looking,

but he was also sweet, kind and very interesting to talk to. When he informed me, as I dropped him off, that he would "love to do it again soon," I was so surprised that I never even realized that I had begun a new relationship.

I noticed throughout the first few weeks that Jason wasn't aware of how attractive he was. It wasn't just in looks, but in his quiet mannerisms and frequent smiles. He walked around not noticing how girls gawked at him, while I gave them menacing looks and held his hand a little tighter.

He cared about me very much and told me so all the time. He would explain that I should never worry about the other girls, who laughed giddily in his presence, because I was the one he wanted. But nevertheless, when I would hear stories of girls flirting with him while he was out with his friends, I would suddenly be very upset and unsure.

I had always thought of myself as an average-looking person. I know that I am caring and have many good qualities to my personality, but when I went out with my friends, it wasn't a great personality that guys seemed to be looking for. It was the first time I had ever dated someone who was so astoundingly handsome, and I soon realized that I felt as though I just wasn't pretty enough to be Jason's girlfriend.

My insecurities began to affect our relationship. If I felt I didn't look as good as I should when we went out, or when I saw pictures of Jason's beautiful ex-girlfriend, I became moody and quiet, usually spoiling the good time we might have had if I had just relaxed and recognized that Jason loved me for who I was, not what I looked like.

When my uncertainty became apparent to him, he sat me down and looked straight into my eyes.

"I want you to listen to me," he said seriously. "It does not matter what you look like now, or what you will look like ten years from now. I love you because of the millions of little things that make you you—and I always will."

I thought about what he said for a long time, and realized that if someone that I thought was so incredible loved me the way that I was, then I had no reason not to feel the exact same way. It wasn't easy to accept myself the way I was, but from that day on, I made a conscious effort to try—and to be proud of what I looked like. No one else in the world looked exactly like me!

When I began to stop constantly criticizing myself for my shortcomings, I am sure that the happiness I felt was contagious. And when I began to let Jason love me for being me, I know that the smile I wore made me even more beautiful.

# Everyone Has a Boyfriend but Me

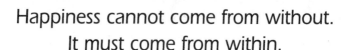

> Happiness cannot come from without.
> It must come from within.
>
> Helen Keller

*Dear Kim,*

*Ever since I started high school everything has changed. Everyone I know is in a relationship but me. They make it look so easy. It hasn't been for me, though. I don't like most of the guys I know, and the one I do like is in a relationship already.*

*I wouldn't be so upset about it except I am starting to feel left out. They all make plans together, and if I am invited I feel like a tagalong. I don't want to get a boyfriend for the wrong reason, but sometimes I am tempted. What should I do?*

This is one of the difficult things about growing up. Things change, and sometimes you feel like you can't catch up. Don't worry, it only seems that way.

I have a good friend who once felt the same way you are feeling now. She began to worry that she would never have a boyfriend. I kept telling her to be patient and just hang in there. She is in college now and we laugh about those days. It isn't like she has had tons of boyfriends, but she certainly hasn't been lonely. She was pickier than some people, but when she did get into a relationship, it was with someone she really liked. She has been with the same guy for three years now, and they are very happy.

This relationship thing is different for everyone. Try not to compare yourself with your friends and you will be much happier.

Remember: You don't have to go looking for love. When it is time, *it will find you.*

# I Wonder

MIRIAM PEREZ

I wonder,
What I could do
Or say
To make him like me.
I wonder,
What or who
I need to be
To be his.
I wonder,
When just being me
Will be enough.

# Why Do All the Girls Like Older Guys Now?

---

♥

---

We are the hero of our own story.

Mary McCarthy

---

*Dear Kim,*

*Why is it that girls all like the same guys? More to the point, why is it that they don't like me?*

*I am a freshman this year, which has really not been fun. I was happy in junior high and, without sounding weird, I was popular, too. Then when I went to high school it was like I disappeared or something. All the girls that used to at least be friends with me started hanging out with older guys and completely ignoring me. These girls and I used to be really good friends. As far as a girlfriend, forget it. They all want to be with an older guy or at least someone who looks older or plays football or basketball with the older guys.*

*I am not a jock—never have been, never will be. It never seemed to matter before, but now it does. I hate this, and I am afraid I will remain girlfriend-less for all the wrong reasons.*

Sometimes life just isn't fair. This is one of those cases. Guys starting high school get a raw deal. Girls have it a lot easier.

Everyone is trying to adjust to a new environment and be accepted into this new scene. Because it is socially acceptable for guys to like girls who are younger than they are, this is a very common scenario. Many of these guys spent the previous year in the same situation you are in now and were waiting for an opportunity to be the older guy. I guess this is something that you, too, can look forward to.

I wish that teenagers weren't so fickle and weren't so harsh when it comes to other people's feelings, but they are. Sometimes, it is like a war zone where everyone is on his or her own, every person for himself or herself.

The girls who used to be your friends probably don't want to hurt you, but they feel that they have to take care of themselves, at all costs. They are under the same pressures you are, to be accepted and to get along in a totally new and foreign environment. The best advice I can give to you is to try to make the best of a bad situation.

First, there must be other kids you can hang out with. Have fun with them. Check out the girls who aren't chasing after the older guys. We often look in the same places, where we have been comfortable before. We join a clique and stay there because it is familiar. Look elsewhere. Try to be aware of the ways you have been close-minded and open up to new groups of people. You may find friends and girlfriends that you never knew existed.

I know a girl who went through something like this. She was rejected by her group of friends and found herself lonely and very hurt. It took a while, but eventually she found another group of friends. Today if you ask her, she can't believe she hadn't hung out with these people before. She felt she was too good for them, and they were not her "type" of people. They are her dearest friends today, and they have so much in common.

We suffer if we are too close-minded about people and groups. I know it is hard in high school to go from one group to another, but I also know the kids who haven't restricted themselves in this way are happier and are the ones who have leadership qualities. By leadership qualities, I mean being in charge of your own life. *You* decide who is worthy of your friendship and who is not. *You* decide whom you like and whom you don't. Don't be swayed by your group or the "popular" kids. These kinds of decisions will give you a real sense of self-worth. They aren't the easiest decisions, but they are the ones that will have the bigger payoffs.

In this way, you begin to have true self-respect. And although your goal to respect and like yourself should be motivated by your own desire for self-love, it can't hurt to tell you—girls love a guy with self-respect.

# Am I Good Enough for Him?

♥
_____

The psychic scars caused
by believing that you are ugly leave
a permanent mark on your
personality.

Joan Rivers
_____

*Dear Kim,*

*I am fifteen years old. I have heard at least a million times that there is* someone for everyone *and other such statements expressing the ideals of love.* There is someone out there waiting for you, it's what's on the inside that matters and beauty is only skin deep. *You're following me here, right?*

*I am not pretty. I am not ugly, but I am by no means a "natural beauty" like I so often hear my sister being described. I am plain.*

*My question is this: How do I know who is "in my league"? You know how you always hear people say, "Well, he is really out of her league" or something dumb like that? How do you know who is and who isn't a realistic possibility?*

*I have a crush on this guy. He isn't the most popular, and he isn't the best looking; he is what I would call average. I happen to think he is great. How do I know that his "average" and my "average" are on the same level? How do I know whether or not he is a long shot?*

I love this question. It really describes what so many people wonder about but don't have the nerve to say out loud.

Hierarchies are funny things. The scale by which people are judged to be better or worse, superior or inferior is a reality that we all have experienced from both sides. In my life I have felt superior about a million times and have felt inferior about a million times. If I were to be honest, I have probably felt inferior 1,001,020 times! My point is that the scale moves back and forth. Some days you will feel confident, and some days you will feel insecure. You are never stuck in one position.

As for your question . . .

Ideally, I would encourage you to pay no attention to this nonsense and if you like him, go for it. But I understand your predicament. Don't give it total power, but be aware that it is one tiny part of the overall equation.

Ask a friend or two what they think. Ask his friend if he thinks "Dan" would want to go out sometime. If you don't want to be that straightforward check it out in more subtle ways: "What do you think of that guy Dan? I heard he liked Sarah. What do you think of that? Would Sarah ever go out with him?"

This is a good way just to measure things and see what others think.

When you begin to have feelings for somebody new, it is a natural and common reaction—no matter what your age—to wonder if you are good enough for that person. You hold the other person in such high esteem and think he or she can do no wrong; that person is perfect in your eyes. Because you do not yet know the other person's flaws and shortcomings (you will!) and you know your own so very well, it makes sense that you would question whether or not you are good enough for him or her. Surely, you think, there are other people out there who would more closely match your crush's level of "perfection." When you find yourself feeling insecure about what you think you have to offer this person, try to be gentle with yourself and reflect on all your positive qualities. Think of all the things the two of you have in common. Most importantly, be yourself. Remember, confidence is very appealing. I think it is one of the most important factors that determines whether or not we are attracted to another person. Know that you *are* good enough.

We all love the movies where outcasts end up getting

the guy or the girl because, once they are given a chance, everyone sees how great they are. The nerd gets the girl or the girl everyone makes fun of turns out to be the real beauty. The point is . . . we all have it in us, including you!

# I'm Losing My Confidence

*Dear Kim,*

*My girlfriend of seven months broke up with me, and I am kind of a mess. She had a way of making me feel so good about myself. When we were going out my grades got better, my parents and I got along better, and everything seemed to go smoother. I felt like I was all the things she saw me as. She would tell me how smart I was and how funny and how handsome and so on. She had a way of making me believe all those things. Now that she is gone I feel the opposite of all that. I feel like I am worthless and unlovable. I feel like she found out who I really was and she left me.*

*I'm feeling pretty down on myself.*

Being in love is like what you described. You feel like you are more than you have ever been. The truth is that you *are* those things that you felt. It is just easier to feel them when you are in love. Let me try to explain.

We are all truly wonderful people. We are, in fact, perfect. When we are in love, our hearts open up, and we are able to get in touch with that part of ourselves. When the other person leaves us, for whatever reason, we do not cease being the wonderful people we are. We just stop having the open heart that allows us to experience our wonderfulness.

One of the big goals in life is to have our hearts open without having to be in love. This is why you hear so much about self-love and self-esteem.

Try to at least know in your mind, if not your heart, that you are all the wonderful things you thought you were. Try to begin to have that kind of self-worth. Also, know that this will get easier with time. You have to re-establish your sense of self, and that will take some time. It gets easier each time you go through this. The first time is the most difficult.

Just remember that she did not make you wonderful. She only helped you to see that you are.

# *I'm Not Pretty Enough for Him*

♥

## Taking joy in life is a woman's best cosmetic.

Rosalind Russell

*Dear Kim,*

*I have a big crush on this guy Josh. I have liked him for a long, long time. Problem is my girlfriend likes him, too. She says she liked him before me, but I know this isn't true. Anyway, I am writing to you because I am afraid he is going to like her when he finds out she likes him. She is much prettier than I am. I am afraid I will lose both of them at once.*

It sounds to me like you need to put some time into loving yourself. Your situation is a good example of why it is so important.

First of all, guys don't just like girls because of how they look. I won't lie to you—it is part of the equation, but by no means all of it. Self-confidence and self-respect play a huge part in the outcome also, and girls happen to be prettier when they have confidence. So . . . my advice would be to dedicate some time to yourself.

Do things that will build your confidence. Exercise, take a dance class, read, do things that you love to do. If you care about yourself and spend time working on yourself, you experience your own power. It's about giving yourself some energy and attention. This is very exciting and a very big confidence builder.

If you do these things, you won't feel like you do now. I promise.

As for your friend, I would have a talk with her—a nice talk in which you just tell her honestly how you feel. After all is said and done, remember: Friendship is always more important than a crush. The two of you should remind yourselves that your friendship will more than likely outlive many crushes. Remember what is most important.

# Dreaming of Me

MIRIAM PEREZ

He's out there somewhere,
Waiting for me just like I'm waiting for him.
Feeling the same things I'm feeling right now,
Thinking there may never be an end to the loneliness,
The longing,
The void that grows with each passing minute.
He's out there,
Somewhere,
Dreaming of me.

*Two*

# Falling in Love

*Love is but the
discovery of ourselves in
others, and the delight
in the recognition.*

Alexander Smith

# *Falling in Love*

♥

Falling in love consists merely in
uncorking the imagination and
bottling the common sense.

Helen Rowland

Ask people what they think it means to fall in love and each and every person will have a different answer. I, myself, have often wondered why it is called "falling in love" instead of "opening to love" or "growing in love." But it is love we are talking about, and one thing everyone does agree on is that love is a powerful force. Those of you who have already been in love know that there is a certain sense of losing control. This can be wonderful and frightening at the same time. How will it turn out? Will the other person return my love? Will he or she love me forever and never hurt me? What if I stop loving him or her? There are a thousand questions and no guarantees. The only thing about love that is constant is that it will run its own course. You can't control it, and, once you feel it, you can't stop it. Let yourself enjoy it. It is like a ride at an amusement park: The more you are able to let go and trust that it will work out okay, the more you will enjoy the ride.

# The Perfect Guy?

KATIE BRENNAN

The love we give away is the
only love we keep.

Elbert Hubbard

I met Kyle the summer before we started our junior year in high school. He was unlike any other guy that I had ever dated. Kyle was different. For some reason, I was drawn to his crooked grin and his dancing, light-blue eyes. I loved the feel of my fingers running through his unruly auburn hair, and I loved it when he enclosed his arms around me and pulled me close. Not only was he different on the outside, but also on the inside. Kyle was the most caring, thoughtful and wonderful guy that I had ever met. He never ceased to make me laugh, and he always listened to my trivial problems and would offer me a shoulder to cry on if I needed one. I thought I was the luckiest girl in the whole world. That is, until fall rolled around.

My friends were all dating the school hunks. You know the type: blond hair and a varsity letter or two. Or three. I felt inferior to my friends and I was beginning to feel more and more ashamed of my relationship with Kyle.

One day, I was walking down the hall with a new friend, Angela, when those familiar arms enclosed my waist and I smelled the familiar scent of his cologne. Instead of feeling the flutter of pride and happiness I had felt all summer, a shiver of nervousness and embarrassment traveled through me. I quickly pulled away.

"I've got to go," I told Kyle and practically ran down the hallway, dragging Angela with me. We stopped to catch our breath at the end of the hall.

"Why do you go with him, anyway?" Angela looked disgusted. "I mean, do you ever take a look at what he wears? And it's like, get a haircut! If I were you, I'd be mortified to even be seen with him! I swear, Katie, you can do so much better. . . ."

As Angela babbled on about all of Kyle's faults I began to think, *Wow, maybe she's right. Maybe they're all right.* My friends had been trying to persuade me to break up with Kyle ever since school began. The more I thought about it, the more I was convinced that Kyle was nothing but an embarrassing accessory that had gone way out of style. I had made my decision.

When I got home, I picked up the phone and dialed Kyle's number. "Hi, Mrs. Lawlor? This is Katie . . . yeah, I'm fine . . . well, she's great, too . . . uh-huh . . . um, can I speak with Kyle, please? Thanks." I nervously licked off my strawberry lipgloss as I listened to Mrs. Lawlor call her son.

Kyle got on the phone. "Katie, hi!" he exclaimed. "I haven't talked to you all day. You'll never guess what happened in Physics Club today—"

"No, wait, Kyle. I have to tell you that . . . well . . ." I took a deep breath and spit it out. "I don't think that it's a good idea for us to be a couple anymore. It's just not working out. Kyle, it was fun, but it's over."

Silence.

"Kyle? I hope you're okay with this, because I mean, I—"

"No, I'm not okay. I know exactly why you're breaking up with me. You're shallow and superficial, Katie, just like all those other girls. Well, you're free to go out with all the jocks you want. I hope they make you happy, because I guess I sure wasn't enough."

*Click.*

I placed the receiver back in the cradle, numbly walked over to my quote calendar and habitually flipped to that day's page. I read the quote once, then twice, then again. What was written on it moved me in a way I still cannot explain.

*Love is a little blind. When we love someone dearly, we unconsciously overlook many thoughts.*
—*Beatrice Saunders*

Suddenly, I saw my life in a totally different light. Tears cascaded from my eyes. I buried my head in my pillow and thought about what he had said. Kyle was right. I was a terrible person. Guilt pricked at me like a thorn. All those times I had brushed him off in embarrassment . . . why? *Why?* Because he wasn't blond and built? Because he didn't have a flashy car or play a varsity sport? The stupidity of it all became so clear to me. Why hadn't I seen it before? I was wrong, and I knew what I had to do.

The next morning at school, I walked up to Kyle's locker. He looked at me and said nothing. I took a shaky breath and began: "Kyle, I am so sorry. I was wrong in breaking up with you just because I cared too much about what other people thought. You're right. I'm shallow and superficial and dumb, and if you never want to look at me again I wouldn't blame you. But please, can I please just maybe have—"

"Another chance?" he asked.

I nodded. Kyle cupped my chin in his hand. "Katie, I guess I knew that this was going on ever since we started school. I always have been afraid that I would lose you. I forgive you, and of course you can have another chance."

I threw my arms around his neck, and once again I felt warmth and pride come over me—this time without the stab of humiliation.

My boyfriend Kyle. You know, he's unlike other guys. My boyfriend Kyle possesses one of the greatest qualities any person could have: He is forgiving.

# Is This Love?

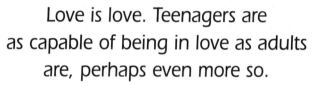

Love is love. Teenagers are
as capable of being in love as adults
are, perhaps even more so.

Kimberly Kirberger

*Dear Kim,*

*I have a question. I am in my third relationship. I thought for sure that I was in love with my first boyfriend, Chris. My mom used to tease me and say I didn't have a clue what love was. Then when I fell in love with Daniel, I thought she was right. I hadn't been in love with Chris, but this time it felt like the real thing. My mom continued to make her little comments.*

*Now I am in a new relationship, and I am much older. This time it feels different than it did with Chris or Daniel. I really feel like this time it is the real thing, but I can't stand the idea of being wrong again.*

*Of course, my mom continues to insist that I am not*

*old enough to understand love in a grown-up way. Please help. I'm sick of feeling like I'm always wrong.*

You make many good points with your question.

Throughout this book, you will notice there are questions about love, and there are many different answers about what "it" is.

I don't think there is a good reason to judge the different definitions of what love is. In fact, I think it may help to look at it as "Stages of Love."

The first thing I suggest is to stop making it a black-or-white issue: was love/wasn't love. My guess is that you loved all three boyfriends but in different ways and in different stages. Each time you experience love and/or a relationship, you are going to learn and to grow (hopefully). This being the case, each relationship will be different and hopefully each one a little bit better.

When you are very young it is impossible to understand love the same way older people—including your mother—do.

*However, this does not mean you are not experiencing true love. I think you are!!!!!!!*

Let me explain.

Say it is fishing we are talking about. The first time you go fishing, you throw the hook into the water and hope to catch a fish. The second time, you put a worm on the hook and hope to catch a fish. The third time, you know to go at a certain time of day, use a different kind of bait and fish at the top of the river.

You have more information and more wisdom each time you go fishing. *That doesn't mean that the first time you went, you weren't fishing though, does it?*

It upsets me to hear adults tell teenagers that they don't know what love is. If we were to be completely honest, we would tell you that some of our most wonderful memories of being in love happened when we were teens. Often, what adults remember are the difficulties and the lack of wisdom. But there is also the pure innocence of true love.

Please don't undermine your feelings. The love that you feel for another person, whether it be for your friends, your parents or your first three boyfriends, is something very special.

Love is real, by definition. When it comes into your life, no matter what course it may take, please remember that it is a precious gift.

# You Tell Me

## Kim Llerena

What does it feel like to be in love?

Does it soothe—
like a soft mist dusting your neck,
cooling your shoulders,
relaxing your tensions?

Does it seize—
like an unrelenting grasp over your being,
your smiles and your tears,
your common sense and your emotions?

Does it excite—
starting at your toes and rising to your chest,
then your throat where it holds its breath,
until it can't help but scream?

Does it confuse—
Am I supposed to feel this way?
Does he feel this way? Why does he lead me on?
What is it in those eyes that makes me so flustered?

You tell me.

Does every smile, every glance, every chance meeting
feel like a promise to love you back?
Not because that's what you really think,
but because it's what you need to think
to keep the hope of a fairy-tale romance
from fading?

Does every conversation
linger for days?
Every frame
clear but unreal
in every daydreamy rerun?

You tell me.

Does he consume your mind
day to long-awaited day
until everything has lost its original luster
when he isn't around
to charm the scene?

Does every playful poke
make you float above cloud nine
like you're rising but staying still?
Does every friendly hug
force the corners of your mouth up into a stupid grin?

*Why do my knees become uselessly weak*
*with every meaningless touch—*
*or even when he walks within twenty feet*
*of my 'personal space'?*

You tell me.

Does it always feel like more than just a crush
or a silly infatuation
when he talks to you
just like you would imagine a soul mate would
and laughs at your jokes?

"If it feels like love isn't it love?"

You tell me.

Because what do I know about it?
I'm only a kid, right?
Heck, I've only been in love once or twice.

# I Can't Open Up . . . and Now I've Lost Him

♥

---

Trust enables you to put your deepest feelings and fears in the palm of your partner's hand, knowing they will be handled with care.

Carl S. Avery

---

Dear Kim,

I have a problem. I have just broken up with my boyfriend. I didn't leave him because he wasn't nice to me or he didn't love me enough. In fact, he was the nicest guy I have ever known. The problem is me. I get really scared when someone is nice to me and loves me.

When I first started seeing him, things were fine. I liked him first, and he was reluctant to get involved. Over time, he began to call me more often, wanting to spend more and more time with me.

*The other night he told me he loved me and that he wished I would open up to him. I got really scared because I am uncomfortable being too personal with guys, and I told him if he didn't like me the way I was he could just leave. He said that he feels sorry for me because I am scared of love. He has never been pushy about sex with me or anything . . . this isn't about that. He just wants me to talk about my feelings, and I don't know how. Whenever I try, I just get uncomfortable and I want him to leave.*

*Instead of being honest with him I pushed him away, and now I want him back. What do I do?*

Many people are afraid to get too close to someone. The first thing you need to do is stop beating yourself up for it.

My guess is you have been hurt and matters of the heart are very painful for you.

There are a couple of things you can do.

If you really trust your boyfriend, he can help you to explore your feelings.

The idea is to *feel* the feelings rather than run from them.

It is possible that something happened to you that is very painful, and in that case you might want to see a therapist. There are many young people in therapy today. It is not what some people think—that it's just for people who are mentally unstable. Therapy is for anyone who wants to learn about himself or herself—and learn to enjoy life and love more.

When I started therapy I learned that I, too, have a difficult time trusting people. It is hard for me to open up and receive love from others. Since going to therapy and working on these things, my relationship with my husband is much better.

The fact that you don't want to lose Dan and you are seeing that your fear makes you unhappy tells me you are ready to change. I want you to be able to enjoy love rather than be frightened of it. Promise me you will deal with these issues and not let them cheat you of a life filled with love. Everyone deserves to be happy.

# Stone by Stone

RACHEL BENTLEY

I have a wall you cannot see
Because it's deep inside of me.
It blocks my heart on every side
And helps emotions there to hide.
You can't reach in,
I can't reach out,
You wonder what it's all about.

The wall I built that you can't see
Results from insecurity.
Each time my tender heart was hurt
The scars within grew worse and worse.
So stone by stone,
I built a wall,
That's now so thick it will not fall.

Please understand that it's not you—
Continue trying to break through.
I want so much to show myself
And love from you will really help.

So bit by bit,
Chip at my wall,
Till stone by stone it starts to fall.

I know the process will be slow—
It's never easy to let go
Of hurts and failures long ingrained,
Upon one's heart from years of pain.
I'm so afraid
To let you in;
I know I might get hurt again.

I try so hard to break the wall,
But seem to get nowhere at all.
For stone upon each stone I've stacked,
And left between them not a crack.
The only way
To make it fall is imperfections in the wall.

I did the best I could to build
A perfect wall, but there are still
A few small flaws, which are the key
To breaking through the wall to me.
Please use each flaw
To cause a crack
To knock a stone off of the stack.

For just as stone by stone was laid
With every hurt and every pain,
So stone by stone the wall will break
As love replaces every ache.
Please be the one
Who cares enough
To find the flaws, no matter what.

# I'm in Love with Love!

## Love is love's reward.

John Dryden

*Dear Kim,*

*Ever since my first relationship, I have been in one relationship after the other. Before I leave the guy I am with, I find another one. I just go from one guy to the next. My friends are starting to really hassle me about it, and I know they are right. The thing is, I hate being alone, and I love being in love. I am with someone now, and I know it is over. My girlfriend is begging me to leave him and spend some time alone. She is afraid I am getting a bad reputation as well as creating bad habits.*

The good thing is that you see what you are doing. So now all you need to do is change the behavior. It isn't easy, I know, but it won't be nearly as bad as you think. Love is about you and someone else liking each other, caring for one another and being attracted to each other. It isn't about filling a need or replacing one boyfriend with another.

You need some time to be by yourself and think about things.

Why do you lose interest in every guy you are with?

Why do you always have to be with someone?

What would happen if you were alone?

It is possible that you are addicted to love. There is an actual addiction to the high you get when you first get involved with someone. Then when that cools off, those who are addicted need to find that feeling with someone else.

It also sounds like you are afraid to feel your feelings. If you have a guy lined up to run to, then you don't have to feel the pain of ending a relationship. If you are always with someone, then you don't have to be with yourself.

The fear is always worse than the reality. Feeling your feelings is how you become real. When we allow ourselves to feel pain, fear and sadness, then we can also feel joy, courage and happiness. We also begin to know ourselves and feel whole.

You see, you are really just running from yourself. I don't know what you think, but I think it is safer to hang out with yourself than it is to hang out with a new guy every week. When you look at it like that, it makes sense, doesn't it?

I really hope this works out for you because I can tell you are ready to make the changes that are going to make you a happier person.

# She's Been Hurt, and Now She Won't Love

♥

Tears may be dried up, but
the heart—never.

Marguerite de Valois

*Dear Kim,*

*There is this girl I love and it is so sad. She loves me, too, but she is afraid I will hurt her because she has been hurt before.*

*How do I let her know that I would never hurt her? I love her so much.*

What a sweet guy you are. The sad thing is that we can't guarantee another person that we will never hurt him or her. We can be someone who handles difficult situations with more kindness, but we can't promise that there won't be difficult situations. We can love other people so much that it seems totally impossible that we would ever hurt them. *But,* it is up to her to trust *herself* by knowing that no matter what happens, she will recover. She has to know that life and love are filled with both pain and happiness. None of us can promise others that we will *never* hurt them. She has to know that love sometimes hurts, and that is the chance we all take.

What about you? You are hurting right now but somehow you know you will survive. You are willing to take the risk. Remind her of that. Let her know that pain builds our muscle. It actually makes our heart stronger each time we allow it to happen without fighting it.

We have to remember that love doesn't come with a guarantee, but that shouldn't stop us.

To you I say . . . be patient, always stay as sweet as you are, and if she doesn't come around I am sure there are girls who would love to be with you.

Try not to let hurt make you put up walls against love.

Hurt isn't the worst thing in the world. It is a great teacher; it softens and strengthens the heart and increases your capacity to love.

The worst thing is to close yourself off to love . . . now that would be unbearable.

# The Pit of Love

JENNIFER HADRA

I fixed my eyes upon the pit
And vowed to stay away.
And yet the blackness called to me,
From where I wished to stay.

They say love's one man's folly
And another's key to fame.
But love was not an issue,
I hated the crying games.

Still, I wandered toward the pit,
It held a strange allure.
It proved a place of mystery
I'd never been before.

Up to the edge I crept,
Looking into the abyss.
Though I knew not what awaited me,
This chance I could not miss.

I lived a sheltered, quiet life;
I longed to risk it all.
I took one more step forward,
'Twas there I took the fall.

I tried to grab onto the edge,
Regretting my new fate.
Instead I kept on falling;
My efforts were in vain.

Although I landed softly,
I sensed a bruise or scar.
But those were often made
In matters of the heart.

However, doubt consumed my mind,
"Would he be like the last?"
Until at length I felt a touch,
It swept the doubt I'd cast.

His strong hands pulled me close to him.
As one we climbed above.
I realized I had fallen safe
Into the arms of love.

# My Special Someone

KRISTINE LEE

Love isn't like a reservoir.
You'll never drain it dry. It's much
more like a natural spring. The longer
and farther it flows, the stronger
and deeper and clearer
it becomes.

Eddie Cantor

I believe in love. I believe that there is a special person out there just for you or in this case just for me. Every night I would gaze up at the stars and wish for my love to appear in my life as soon as possible. My stars came through for me when I least expected them to.

Justin had recently moved to my neighborhood from Canada, and, luckily for me, he moved in right next door. The first time I saw him, I knew. He was an artist, a romantic and an idealist.

He attended the same school as I did and appeared to be shy, belonging to his own private world. Maybe that was why I liked him. I don't know. All I knew was, since I met him, I was dressing nicer and when I was near him, my heart beat faster.

Carmen Tan, the richest girl in school, had a birthday party, and everyone in our class was invited. The only condition was that we had to come with a partner or we would not be allowed in. Immediately, I thought of Justin. This would be easy. He had to have a partner also, and I was almost positive that he didn't have a girl-friend. I decided I would ask him after class. The moment presented itself when I was standing next to him in the hall, but as I drew in my breath to ask him, my knees went weak, and it was all I could do to walk. I chickened out.

I ended up going with a guy named Michael Sim. He was convinced he was the perfect guy for me: my own special someone. But all evening I ignored him and just stared at Justin and his date Natalie. It was martyrdom at its best.

The end of the school year approached, and there was another dance . . . and another chance. I felt so stupid about not being able to ask him the last time that I was too scared to even consider asking him this time.

I did get my chance, though. One night he invited me to his house to help him with some physics problems. As I hung up the receiver, my hands grew clammy and my heart hammered against my rib cage. After changing my clothes one hundred times and making sure everything was perfect with my hair and makeup, I proceeded to go to his house.

Throughout the night, I forced myself to not stare at him. It was very difficult. Very. We had finished a set of problems when he suggested a break. I put down the pencil and started down the stairs for a Coke when all of a sudden Justin grabbed my wrists, turned me around and kissed me on the cheek. My face grew hot, my goosebumps stood tall, and I froze into an icy statue.

He kissed me. Justin! The one I thought of day and night.

"Kris, I like you!" His words flew out in a steady torrent.

For the first time all night I looked into his eyes—deep into their depths. I touched his soul. Then I turned and ran down the stairs and out the door onto the street into my house and onto my bed.

Till this day I do not know what possessed me. I actually ran away from the situation I had been dreaming of. What was I doing?

Justin never spoke to me after that. The next day at school, he tried to make eye contact with me, but I purposely avoided him. I just could not face him. Not after the way I had acted.

Soon after, he left for Paris to further his studies. I heard he found another and is engaged.

As for me, I'm now with Michael Sim. Life is funny that way. I guess he was my special someone after all.

# Help . . .
# I'm Afraid of Falling!

♥

> We are always afraid to start
> something that we want to make
> very good, true and serious.
>
> Brenda Ueland

*Dear Kim,*

*I was dating this guy Joe. Then another guy whom I liked asked me out. So I went out with him. Since I had no commitment to either, there was a short period of time when I was seeing both of them. That wasn't working for me, so I broke it off with Joe and started seeing only Tim. At first Tim came on a bit strong and it kind of scared me, so I asked him if he would slow down a bit. The cool thing was . . . he did. Now things are really good between us. So you might be wondering why I am writing to you. This is why: I am starting to fall in love with him and that really scares me. I don't know why, it just does.*

You know, it's funny. When I was young I had girl-friends like you, and I could never understand them. I used to love falling in love, and, for some reason, I was never frightened.

What I am learning as I get older is that a little bit of fear would have been healthy. However, a little bit of my way would help you, too. It is all about balance.

There is nothing wrong with being a little cautious. You want to get to know someone, make sure he or she is trustworthy, kind, etc. But once you have done that and that person passes all the "tests," you want to be able to enjoy the feeling of being in love.

There are no guarantees ever that something is going to turn out exactly the way you want it to—no promises of love without pain. In fact, pain is part of the deal. *But,* what you can rely on is yourself. Each time you get hurt and are able to work it out (with or without him), you will build trust in yourself. As that grows, you will be a happier, more secure person. You will be a person who can enjoy love and all its wonder.

*Three*

# All These New Feelings

*Woe to the man
whose heart has not learned
while young to hope, to love
—and to put its trust
in life.*

Joseph Conrad

# All These New Feelings

♥

## Love is a game that two can play and both win.

Eva Gabor

Between the ages of twelve and eighteen, so many changes take place both physically and emotionally. We hear a lot about the physical changes but not as much about the emotional ones.

Suddenly, you have all these new feelings, and it is up to you to try to figure them out. You start liking the opposite sex. You start loving the opposite sex. You feel things like jealousy, fear and competition with those who yesterday were simply your friends. To make it all more confusing, they are also feeling all these new things.

Let me start by saying it is a very difficult time. Emotions become much more intense than ever before. Suddenly you are looking at yourself in a different way, too. It is like someone put a magnifying glass in front of you and began to point out every single little thing that is wrong with you. You see your faults in a way you have never seen them before. And to make it worse, you think you are the only one with these faults, the only one having these feelings and the only one who will never be understood. This, by definition, is *not fun!*

The following is a little story about Dylan, Lisa, Brad and Ashley:

Dylan is in math class and is very bored. He looks over at Lisa and thinks to himself that she is very pretty. He smiles at her. She smiles back.

After class, Lisa sees her girlfriend, Ashley, and says to her, "I think Dylan likes me." They then rush off to their next class and promise to eat lunch together.

Ashley's friend, Brad, is in her next class and they always sit in the back and talk. She tells him that Lisa thinks Dylan likes her.

Brad is very good friends with Dylan, so he kind of wonders to himself why Dylan hadn't mentioned anything to him. The next time he sees Dylan he asks him.

"So you have a thing for Lisa? Why didn't you tell me?" Brad asks.

Dylan looks at him and says, "What are you talking about? Where did you hear that?" It is obvious that he is upset.

He goes on to question Brad, "Did you hear anything else; what about *her?* Who's spreading this rumor?"

Brad is kind of put off by how upset Dylan is and wants to get out of the way before Dylan gets mad at him. He says he'll catch up with him later.

Brad runs into Ashley on his way to lunch and tells

her that Dylan is really mad. Ashley pushes Brad to tell her why and he says, "I think it is because of the rumor that he likes Lisa," Brad says to Ashley. "I guess it isn't true, and he is mad."

Ashley quickly says "bye" and finds Lisa for their lunch "date."

Ashley gently informs Lisa that Brad told her that Dylan doesn't like her. She also tells her that he is kind of mad about the whole thing.

Lisa starts to cry, believing she is ugly and unlovable. She is heartbroken. She spends the whole lunch asking Ashley what is wrong with her.

"Is it my looks? Is it the way I act around guys? Is it because I'm not as popular as he is?" No question is left unasked.

Ashley suggests that she try and make Dylan jealous.

The next day Lisa flirts with every guy she sees, most of all Brad. Brad likes being flirted with. In fact, he likes it so much that he asks Ashley if she thinks Lisa would ever go out with him. Ashley is a little hurt by this because she has always had a secret crush on Brad.

She tells Brad she doesn't think Lisa would go out with him because, honestly, she just couldn't bear the idea. Brad makes a comment about Lisa being a snob anyway and walks off.

After school that day, Brad and Dylan decide girls aren't worth getting upset over.

Lisa calls Brad that night to see if he can shed any light on the Dylan thing and Brad is really cold to her. He is thinking to himself how heartless she is.

Lisa calls Ashley crying because Brad was so mean to her on the phone and, in a moment of guilt, Ashley confesses to Lisa that she hasn't been completely honest with her. She goes on to say that Brad told her that he liked her (Lisa) and that she didn't tell her because she was jealous. Lisa is shocked and asks Ashley to repeat what she said one more time. When Lisa realizes that Brad had a crush on her and Ashley had told Brad that she wouldn't go out with him she gets really mad at Ashley. She says she has to go, but Ashley knows it is because she is mad at her.

Ashley starts crying. This has been the worst day. She feels completely alone.

She decides to call Dylan. She cries and tells him everything that happened to her that day. Suddenly Dylan yells, "Wait a minute. . . . What did you just say?"

Ashley repeats, "When Lisa first told me she liked you. . . ."

Dylan makes her repeat it three times.

"How come no one told me that Lisa liked me?" he asked.

"I thought you knew," Ashley told him. "Brad told me you were mad and that you didn't like Lisa, so why do you care anyway?"

With this news Dylan becomes furious with Brad. He tells Ashley he will call her back, but he needs to call Brad first.

After many more phone calls and lots of tears, it is time for them to call it a night.

They each lie in their beds sad and brokenhearted and wondering: *How did everything get so weird???*

What happened to Lisa, Ashley, Dylan and Brad? Feelings are what happened. New, confusing and scary . . . feelings!!! Don't feel bad, it does get easier. However, I would be lying if I said it gets a lot easier.

I know grown women who are too shy to admit that they have a crush on someone who is a friend. I know grown men who would rather miss out completely on a chance with the one they love than risk being made a fool. So . . . what is the key to making it all run a little smoother?

Whenever possible, use *direct communication.*

If you can, tell someone directly that you like him or her. If you hear a rumor about another person's feelings towards you, ask that person directly if it is true.

Yes, this is extremely difficult. Yes, it is often downright impossible. *But,* if you always try to communicate as directly as possible, then you have a much better chance of avoiding the Dylan-Lisa scenario. And you have a much better chance of enjoying and even *surviving* "all these new feelings."

# The "L" Word

## AMANDA BAILEY

In my sixteen years in this world I've laughed and I've cried, I've tried and I've fallen, I've received and I've lost, I've lived and I've loved. Yet the one thing that keeps me constantly reeling with confusion is the "L" word. Yes, I've come to find that *love,* the most overly exhausted word in the English language, has Amanda Gail Bailey at quite a loss.

As a child, my mind fed off of Disney movies and storybook endings. I dreamed of the day my Prince Charming (taller than I am, dark and handsome, of course) would gallop to my castle upon his white horse, shower me with flowers, come to my window and shout "Amanda! Amanda! Let down your hair," climb up and whisk me away to eternal bliss in a gingerbread house. Hmm . . . my memory seems to have failed me. That's not quite the dream, but it was something of the sort. You may snicker at my childhood fantasies. But Golden Books and *The Wonderful World of Disney* proved to have no false testimonies.

My next phase was preadolescence (enter funeral

procession song). My life was soon filled with braces and acne, the frightful mention of "boy-girl" parties, and gross little weaklings who were suddenly being referred to as "fine guys." Umm . . . did I miss something? What a disappointment! My Cinderella hopes crashed and burned.

I found myself getting excited at the measly proposal notes asking, "Will you go with me? Check yes or no. (And please give this back to my best friend Jerry, not me.)" My new realm of love spanned only from how fast word of my two-day relationship with the new guy was traveling, to which friend I'd grace with the honor of delivering the "breakup" message.

What a relief when the middleman was cut out and actual means of communication were exchanged between members of the male gender and me. Sometime during my freshman year in high school, the words "going out" were quickly replaced by the sophisticated term "dating." I mean, this was serious stuff. By seeing the mass forming of couples that occurred, you'd think the world was coming to an end tomorrow and all parents had given children under the age of sixteen permission to date.

Yet, the older I get, the more I find that I've been blessed (I suppose you could call it that) with a heart that is quick to fall in love. I've learned that there really is a time when you find someone who seems to share the same hopes and dreams as you—someone to whom you give your whole heart. And that is how I've learned the pain of a broken heart. I must admit, for "puppy love" the pain at the time seems never-ending. But soon, you learn to pick up the pieces of your shattered heart, mold them carefully into *almost* what your heart was before (for I've found that once your heart is broken, it's never quite the same), and then become more discerning about which Romeos you tend to fall for.

I've got a lot of life left to live, and love yet to give. Though I could be practical and search for that sensible guy, I'll still turn my head when the thunder of a horse's footsteps comes galloping into my heart. I'm still waiting for my Prince Charming. He's out there somewhere. . . .

# What Is He Thinking?

*Dear Kim,*

*I am more than confused. I have been going out with this guy, on and off, for over two years. Right now it is off, but only because he wants it that way.*

*We were so great together, and I know he loved me a lot: more than anyone he has ever been with. We had some problems, and we broke up. We got back together twice, and the second time we were having a difficult time. I was willing to hang in there, though, because I really loved him.*

*One day, he announced it was over. I took it pretty hard because I still love him. What is really confusing, though, is he seems to have just turned his feelings off. It is like he never felt anything for me.*

*He won't talk to me, he won't return my calls, and this has been going on for months.*

*I still love him, though. What should I do? Please help me to understand why someone would act like this.*

I wish I could say that this is highly unusual behavior, but I can't. Believe it or not, it is rather common.

Simply put, he got hurt and he is determined not to get hurt again.

Maybe he realized it would never work, or maybe he did "just get over you." *But,* if that were the case, he would not be acting like he is.

If someone is really *over* you, they wouldn't *need* to *not* talk to you. There would be no reason to be cruel. When you are *over* someone, you behave apathetically.

As for a solution, I don't know. I guess the best thing would be for you to let go and move on, but that isn't easy, especially when things are so unprocessed, so up in the air.

You could try to write him a letter. In that letter, you could tell him how you feel. *No* blame!! *No* attacking . . . just how you feel.

He might respond, but the bottom line is this: He may not. You may have to let it go.

I know someone who went through this same exact thing. When she got over the guy and started liking someone else, he called her. In this call, he admitted to her that he never stopped loving her, and he wanted to give it another try. She was, however, over him, and they never did get back together. They are friends now, but she will never forget that bittersweet moment when he admitted his feelings. How she would have loved to have known this on the nights she spent crying herself to sleep.

Thus the saying: Love stinks!!!!

# My Friend Stole My Crush

♥

It is true that selfish persons
are incapable of loving others, but
they are not capable of loving
themselves either.

Erich Fromm

*Dear Kim,*

*I am so upset. The other day when I was talking to my girlfriend, I started telling her how much I liked this guy named Alan. She didn't say anything; she just kind of listened and asked questions. It felt good to finally tell someone about this crush I had been keeping to myself for so long.*

*The next day, she had her best friend tell Alan that she liked him, and he agreed to go out with her. If I make a big deal of it, I am afraid she will tell him and they will make fun of me.*

*I am really mad, though. She has done the same thing to other friends of hers. What should I do?*

Well, first of all, I think it would be a good idea to mark her name off your friend list. Unfortunately, there are girls who put guys before friendships. You make your own decision, but I decided long ago that I had no use for friends like this.

Many girls and guys decide who they are going to like based on who their friends like. This makes them feel superior when they are the ones going out with that person. The only reason people behave this way is that they are insecure, and they don't trust their own feelings and attractions.

If I were you, I would calmly tell the girl that you think what she did was pretty lame. You can proceed to tell her how you feel, but try not to let yourself get too upset.

There will be other guys for you, but she will quickly run out of friends if she continues to behave this way.

Another thing to keep in mind is that once you no longer care about her or Alan, she will quickly lose interest, also. My guess is Alan will be available sooner than you think. Maybe then he will be ready for someone who truly likes him.

# Sister

BECCA WOOLF

Sister, sister, where'd you go?
I turned and you weren't there.
You left me for your boyfriend
and I wonder if you care.

Sister, sister, what'd you do?
He was mine, don't you remember?
For all the times I cried to you
on how I'd care forever.

Sister, sister, why'd you lie
and turn your back on me?
I was positive that friendship
had a longer guarantee.

Sister, sister, times have changed
you into . . . I don't know?
And I wonder where my sister went
and why she had to go.

Sister, sister, how are you?
And, who's your friend today?
You swap friends like a deck of cards
and act like it's okay.

Sister, sister, when have friendships
been more at their end?
I'm giving up, I'm letting go
of my sister . . . and my friend!

"When I said, 'I think we should start seeing other people,'
I didn't mean this exact second!"

# I Have to Choose Between Two Guys

---

Getting in touch with your true self
must be your first priority.

Tom Hopkins

---

*Dear Kim,*

*I am in a situation I never thought would happen to me. For the longest time, I was alone without a boyfriend and was scared it would always be that way. Then I got a boyfriend, and I was happy to finally not be alone. Then something happened that confused everything. There was a guy I liked very much before I was with Zach. He didn't like me at the time, and so I moved on. Now that I am with Zach, the guy I liked before likes me. I don't know what to do because I like both of them. I feel that it is wrong to even think about leaving Zach to be with Blake. But I was so in love with Blake and so heartbroken that he didn't like me back. I can't believe that I now have a chance to be with him. Please help.*

I am not a bit surprised that you are feeling confused. Anybody would be. I can remember times when I was in a similar situation and I almost wished that nobody liked me so I wouldn't have to choose. Of course, I said *almost.*

The first thing you need to do is forget everything that has happened and not think about what might happen. Once you have done this, close your eyes for a minute and ask yourself, "How do I feel about Zach?" Then ask yourself, "How do I feel about Blake?" Try to get in touch with your feelings *only.* Don't think about anything else.

If you like one of them more than the other, then that's your answer. If you find that all you are is confused, maybe you need to take a break from both of them until you are able to become clearer about how you feel.

The most important thing is to be true to yourself. It isn't always easy because you get caught up in what people will think, who is more popular and how they will feel. Before you know it, you don't even know how you feel. When we are true to ourselves there is never anything to regret. Just remember to keep it as simple as possible and answer to your heart.

# I'm Unlucky in Love

## Love just happens.
## We don't have to do anything.

Kimberly Kirberger

*Dear Kim,*

*I am in tenth grade. I have a great life. I'm a good athlete, a good student, I have lots of friends, great parents, etc. The only thing is, I have really bad luck when it comes to love. My friends just kind of laugh at me and say I try too hard, which is probably true. Every time I blow it, though, I can't help but think I did something wrong so I need to try harder next time.*

*It feels like whatever the problem is, it just keeps getting worse, not better. What happens is, I get into a relationship with a girl (I have been in three), and, at first, everything is great, and we are in love and having fun. All three times started out so perfect. It was like this is it . . . this is love. Then it starts to cool off a bit, but I know that is to be expected. Then it seems like the more I care about her, the more she pulls away. All three times it ended with me being dumped. Each time they said all this stuff about us being better as friends than as boyfriend/girlfriend, and please can we still be friends and so on.*

*Each time it was so painful, and I didn't quite understand what happened.*

First of all, let me say that when a relationship ends it does not mean that someone did something wrong. There are many things that make a relationship work or not work, and most of them are not in our control.

It sounds like you are a very romantic guy. It sounds like when you fall in love, you fall hard. My guess is that girls love how romantic you are and how open you are to love. Girls *love* guys who aren't afraid to be romantic. Then as the relationship progresses, it is possible that it gets to be too much for them. Perhaps you become overbearing. Maybe you come on so strong that it is scary for them. Maybe it becomes a *need* thing instead of a *want* thing.

One of the biggest "confusions" in love is the difference between loving someone and needing someone. You have to ask yourself, "When I say, 'I love you,' am I saying, 'I care about you and I think you are a great person,' or am I saying, 'I really need you and I need you to love me'?"

Of course, we want the person we love to return that love. But when it becomes so important that everything we are doing is simply to win that person's love, then we need to take a closer look.

The balance of love in relationships is a very delicate thing. If one person is more in love, more in need and more attached, it is scary for the other person. This can often be the beginning of the end. This is why self-love and self-respect play the most important parts in any relationship. It is important to stay centered, to always remember that another person is not responsible for our happiness. It is important to be able to pull back when we get the message that we are coming on too strong.

You said that the girls wanted to be friends with you. Why don't you ask them to tell you what happened? Explain that you just want to be able to understand, and you would like them to be as honest as possible.

Don't give up. Maybe the chemistry just wasn't there and something better awaits you. You sound like a sweet guy, and I am sure you will have a great relationship when the time is right.

# Oh, No . . . She Wants to Have a "Talk"!

*Dear Kim,*

*One of the hardest things about being a guy is this whole love thing.*

*We're supposed to be all strong and together, and yet we are as scared as girls are. I wish guys talked about love and relationships more, but it is considered a sign of weakness if you want to discuss your "crush" with the guys. Let's face it, you'd get made fun of.*

*My problem is, I am clueless. I don't know how to make a relationship work. And I get really freaked out when my girlfriend says she wants to talk.*

*For some reason, I always think it's going to be about my having done something wrong. I just don't feel comfortable analyzing everything.*

I love this question. And you are right: It *is* hard for guys. I have a couple of ideas, though.

Have girls as friends. Girls make great friends for guys and vice versa. Girls love to talk about relationships. They love to talk to guys about relationships because guys can give them insight that girls can't. Everyone benefits. (Don't think for a minute that it is weird to have girls for friends.)

The other thing you can do is talk more with your girlfriend—but not just when things are strained. When things are going great, talk about it. You can even ask her questions about your relationship and how to make it work better. *Girls love this.*

"Justin and I spend all of our free time together, we go out every weekend, and we talk on the phone for hours. We're getting along so much better since we broke up!"

# This Guy Is Spreading Rumors About Me

♥
_____

I'm not afraid of storms, for
I'm learning how to sail my ship.

Louisa May Alcott
_____

*Dear Kim,*

*Okay, there is this guy, and he started telling all his friends that he liked me. He had his friend, Greg, ask me if I wanted to go out with him. I was nice and everything, but I said no because I didn't want to go out with him for a couple of reasons.*

*The next day at school, he started telling everyone that we did go out and that he did stuff with me. I haven't even talked to this guy for more than thirty seconds, let alone anything else.*

*I am really mad because I am afraid people will believe him.*

*What do I do?*

Do you have peer mediation at your school? If you do, I would have to suggest using it for this one. Make him sit in a room with you and call him on it. Make him say out loud that nothing happened between the two of you except that he asked you out and you said no. I would then insist that he put it into writing (if they let you do that). Tell him you won't ever use it unless he starts spreading stuff again.

If you don't have peer mediation, I would try to set something up like it, perhaps with a guidance counselor. I believe this is a serious offense and it needs to be stopped. I think other kids need to see that this isn't the way to deal with rejection. A counselor can require that he attend a meeting where all three of you are present. I would push for something that forces him to look you in the eye and cop to what he's doing and make him tell the truth.

In the meantime, just hold on to your courage and your heart and know that you have done nothing wrong. Try to let it roll off your back when you hear stuff being said.

The more you freak out about it, the bigger it gets, so stay calm and put your energy into solving the problem.

# Alone

## BECCA WOOLF

I didn't want to admit it,
It was easier to lie,
And hide the hurt and emptiness,
To smile instead of cry.
I didn't want to face the fact,
My life is full of pain,
And I long to stop my bleeding heart,
And maybe smile again.
'Cause I feel oh-so-forgotten,
So betrayed and so alone,
Without a trace of forgiveness,
And no soul to call my own.
I didn't want to admit the fact,
I cannot spread my wings,
And my happiness has melted,
Into tears and other things.
It's hard for me to hide the fact,
My wishes have no home,
And return to anguish,
Bow my head and cry alone.

# I'm a Sensitive Guy

*Dear Kim,*

*You know, guys get a bad rap. Everyone thinks we are so coldhearted and that all we want is one thing. This isn't true. Not for me anyway. I am so in love with my girlfriend. I'm crazy about her. She is so beautiful, so sweet, funny and really a strong person. She doesn't take any bull from me, and yet I know she loves me.*

*The thing is, when one of us gets hurt, it is usually me. She doesn't hurt me on purpose, but she can be cold sometimes.*

*I don't have anyone I feel I can talk to about this stuff. I get my feelings hurt all the time, and I have to kind of go through it all by myself.*

*I just want to say it is not always one-sided . . . and guys get hurt, too.*

Good point. We do think of guys as being the tough ones . . . or the rigid ones or the ones who want one thing only or the ones who do the hurting. There is even some pressure for guys to be that way. Guys often feel it is expected of them to be tough and even mean sometimes.

As for solutions to your problem: One great idea is for you to get a girl friend. A friend who is a girl. You can call her and talk about your feelings, and she will understand and love you for it.

I think all guys feel more than they get credit for. I think it is hard for guys because they believe they aren't supposed to have all those feelings. But if you are alive and you are human, you have *all* those feelings. So, even though it is true that guys put up a more rigid front, all guys cry and feel hurt and want to be loved. Some admit it more than others, and that is the *only* difference.

Give yourself a break.

Get a friend who will understand and who you can talk to.

Know you are not the only one.

By the way . . . girls love a sensitive guy!!!

*Four*

# There Is a First Time for Everything: Love Is the Part of Us That Is Real

*Perhaps loving something is the only starting place there is for making your life your own.*

Alice Kollier

# A First Time for Everything

A journey of a thousand miles
begins with a single step.

Confucius

Your first crush, first love, first date, first kiss and first breakup are experiences you will never forget. I remember very little about my teenage years, but I can tell you the name of my first boyfriend, how old I was when I received my first kiss and all the details of my first heartbreak.

When we are in love, life has an extra sparkle to it. Things seem more real, and all our experiences are enhanced by it.

Things change between the time of your first crush and your first date. You change, you mature and you think differently about what this love thing is all about. There is no need, however, to belittle any part of your experience. No need to laugh and say, "I can't believe I used to think I was in love with that Bobby guy." As I will say many times in this book, all our experiences are important because they are all for our learning. They are stages in a very precious process—the process of learning how to love.

So whether you have already experienced these firsts or are just beginning the process, treat them with respect. These firsts will help shape who you are and who you become.

Remember, love is a teacher, a friend and always a gift.

Enjoy!!!

I highly recommend keeping journals. It will be so much fun to look back on all this some day, and it also is very helpful in teaching you about yourself.

# First Time

## JANE WATKINS

In looking back I realize
The first time is a measure
I'll use to weigh my memories
That tomorrow I will treasure.

First kiss, first date, first phone call
First one to hold my hand
First time to feel the kind of love
I hardly understand.

Yet after careful viewing
If it won't hold up to light
I'll have another "first time"
To try and get it right.

# I'm Afraid She'll Reject Me . . .

♥

One makes mistakes; that is life.
But it is never a mistake
to have loved.

Romain Rolland

*Dear Kim,*

*There is this girl. . . . I like her so much. I want to call her and ask her out, but I am really afraid. I am afraid she might say no, and I am also afraid if she does say no and it gets around, other kids will make fun of me. I would be so embarrassed if it turned out that way. I also know if I don't ask, then I will never know.*

Life and love are all about taking risks. This is the way it is. I get hundreds of letters from teens who are in the same situation as you are: scared to tell another of their feelings . . . scared the feelings won't be mutual.

I believe in telling people how you feel rather than keeping it inside. Love is to be shared. One of my favorite quotes says, "Love isn't love till you give it away." What good are your feelings for her if you don't share them with her? If she doesn't like you in return, yes, it will hurt, but then you can move on.

Just remember, whenever we tell other people how we feel, they don't owe us anything in return. They don't even *have* to tell us how they feel if they don't want to.

This is important because if you approach someone with the attitude that she owes you, you will scare that person off . . . big time. When you tell someone you have feelings for her or that you are attracted to her, make sure you do it in a respectful way. If you ask her out and she says, "no thanks," be civil and end on a nice note. Trust me, it is never to your advantage to get weird or to act mean. You just end up looking like a jerk. If you are rejected, go to your friends for support.

One of the harshest things about being a teenager is dealing with friends who act cruel. Being laughed at, talked about and made fun of is awful by anyone's standards. If you want to reduce the chances of being laughed at, don't tell anyone but her. Ask her to keep it between the two of you. Of course, if she says "yes," that means she will only tell her best friend, but it gives you much better odds.

Remember: There is a good chance she will say "yes," and all she will be telling her friends is how cute you are or how happy she is that you guys are going out.

If you don't ask, you'll never know. Trust me, the risk is worth it.

# I Misjudged a Great Guy

♥

Loves cures people,
both the ones who give it, and
the ones who receive it.

Karl Menninger

*Dear Kim,*

*I am in eighth grade, and I have gone to school with the same people for many years now. I haven't ever had a boyfriend, but there is somebody that I like. The problem is that I haven't been very nice to this guy because I used to think he was a creep. (What did I know?) Now that I like him I feel really strange telling him because I feel bad about not being nice to him before.*

*He has started being nicer to me lately, so I am hoping that he isn't holding a grudge, but how can I be sure?*

Ahhh . . . love is great. It is proof that our judgments of other people are simply that—our judgments.

So, you used to think this guy was a creep. There is the possibility that he has matured and changed and therefore become more attractive . . . but there is also the possibility that you are looking at him differently.

Start by being nice to him and letting him know that you no longer think he is a creep. When the time is right, you can invite him to a party or invite him to go with you and some friends to a movie.

If and when he asks you about the way you used to treat him, just tell him that you are sorry and you can see now that you misjudged him. This is much better than trying to defend yourself by telling him that he *was* a creep, but he isn't anymore.

I hope things work out for you guys, but even more important, I hope that this helps all of us to remember that we never know when we are treating someone badly if tomorrow that person will hold the key to our hearts.

# I'm Scared to Kiss Him

♥

All life represents a risk,
and the more lovingly we live our
lives the more risks we take.

M. Scott Peck

*Dear Kim,*

*I am pretty sure my boyfriend wants to kiss me and I definitely want to kiss him. The thing is, I am really scared because I have never kissed a boy before. I know this sounds really stupid, but do you have any advice for me?*

Yes, I do. The most important thing is to enjoy it. Kissing is absolutely wonderful, if you are kissing the right person. If you are kissing someone you like a lot or love, it is wonderful. And if you are doing it because you want to and not because of some external pressure, then it is the best.

There are no rules for kissing. There is no special way you have your lips or certain way to move your tongue. It is a very natural thing. So, if you relax and remember that this is something you are sharing with another person, then you will be fine. Don't try to seem experienced by acting like you have done this before. Just be comfortable because you have nothing to prove. Also, remember that even if he has kissed before, he hasn't kissed *you* before, so it is a first for him, too.

Try not to feel self-conscious and try to help put him at ease. It is okay to even let him know that you are a little nervous.

Just remember, you only have your first kiss once, so do your very best to enjoy it.

# I'm Graduating from High School . . . and I've Never Even Been Kissed

♥

One is taught by experience to put a
premium on those few people who
can appreciate you for what you are.

Gail Godwin

*Dear Kim,*

*I am a senior in high school and have already picked
where I am going to college. I get good grades and have
lots of great friends.*

*The problem is, I have never had a boyfriend, I have
never been on a date and I have never even been kissed.
It is very awkward for me when my girlfriends start talking about guys, and I can't relate. They don't hassle me*

*about it, which, in a way, makes me feel even worse . . .*
*like they, too, are embarrassed for me. I want to at least*
*kiss a guy before I go to college, so I won't be perceived as*
*a freak. How do I do this?*

You are a smart girl, so I don't need to tell you that to
kiss a guy simply to change how you are perceived is not
the right reason to do so, nor is it the way you want to
begin this wonderful journey. Everybody follows his or
her own path where love is concerned.

I had a close friend in high school who was in the
same position as you are. She never had a boyfriend in
high school, nor had she ever been kissed. She was
really pretty, and would despair over why she had never
been kissed. She felt like a "freak" for not having kissed
anyone, but could never bring herself to just "hook up"
with any old high-school guy.

She sure did show us all how it was done where good
grades were concerned, though. She was accepted to a
really good college where—wouldn't you know it?—she
met some great guys! When I would drive up to her college to visit her on weekends, I was blown away by all
the guys she had clamoring for her attention. I, of
course, held on to my *high-school* boyfriend, making me
the "freak" amidst all the fun and frivolity of the college
flirting and dating scene.

Come to think of it, she never really had a very serious

boyfriend in college, either. How could she choose between all the good-looking, talented and intelligent guys she met? She simply had fun, enjoyed the attention and stayed focused on school.

I now understand why the college guys were crazy for her. She had such a strong sense of identity by the time she entered college. She didn't need a guy, and was actually happy without one. When we were all so busy chasing and being chased by the boys in high school, she was getting to know herself, taking time to pursue her interests and figuring out what she wanted to do with her life.

When it is your time it will happen to you, too. Stay true to yourself. When you do kiss someone or find yourself with a boyfriend, do it for you. And don't forget to have fun!

# First Kiss

RON CHENG

It's a beautiful day, the summer before I start seventh grade. For Dee, it's the summer before eighth grade.

I'm watching TV. *Geraldo* is on. The guests argue about their unfaithful husbands or wives, while their wives or husbands deny all of the accusations of infidelity. Suddenly, Dee plops down next to me on the couch, coming from the bathroom. She nuzzles very close to me and rests her head on my shoulder, complaining about how bony it is. I tell her to shut up. I feel very conscious of her head on my shoulder, and then I feel conscious of her staring at me. I look at her and smile.

"What's up?" I ask, confused.

"Nothing," she answers, shaking her head.

She nuzzles even closer to me, and I feel awkward. Her arm slides in between my arm and my body, and she clings to me. A billion thoughts race through my head and then all of a sudden . . . nothing. I feel her staring at me, the heat of her face close to mine. I look at her and I see three eyes. She looks straight into my eyes, pinning me with her gaze, locking my eyes with hers.

"Don't you wanna kiss me?" she asks sweetly.

My mouth drops open, and I quickly close it, realizing that it was not the right look to give off. I start to sweat a little. What's worse, I feel her arms snake around my neck. I glance down for a second, sensing an awkwardness, like she doesn't know what she's doing. I look up again into her big green eyes. Her confidence suddenly blows me away and I am intimidated. Time ceases to pass in minutes or even seconds . . . but in milliseconds. Actually, the only time that exists is measured by the small movements that she makes.

A smile slowly forms on her lips.

I start to blush, feeling my blood rush into my cheeks and I feel stupid, like I don't know what I'm doing, which I don't. And in that moment I curse her for making me feel stupid; she knows what she's doing to me.

I have to do something. Her next move might be an embarrassing question, like, "Do you not know how to kiss or something?" or "Are you a prude?" or "What's wrong with you, boy?" She's too close to me. She's moving too fast for me. She's too close to my face! She's too intimidating. She's too . . . cute!

She stops smiling.

*Oh no! What's she thinking now? I'm so stupid! I should've done something! She thinks I'm a prude! I am! So what?!?!? So, I'm a prude. Give me a break! Give . . . me . . . a break!*

She wets her lips.

*Whoa.*

Her face inches closer.

*Oh man.* Only a breath away from my face now, I see her lips form a smile before she presses hers to mine.

Slow, soft and sweet. Only her arms around me keep me from flying.

After what seems like a few minutes, she stops kissing me and looks up. Her emerald eyes sparkle and she smiles. She giggles and says that I'm cute. I stare at her. She nuzzles back against me and watches TV. I sit there, staring at her, dumbfounded . . . with a stupid smile pasted on my lips.

*Wow.*

# The Kiss

### ALLISON FORSTER

It happened so quickly
The world must have shook.
I'd always hoped it would happen
Like it does in a book.

He looked at me softly
and then touched my hair.
I felt so special
Like he really did care.

He leaned over slowly
My heart upped its pace.
Right at that moment
We were face to face.

When his lips touched mine
I thought I would melt.
His kiss was the sweetest thing
I have ever felt.

"Your top lip kisses really nice, but I think your bottom lip still has feelings for your ex-boyfriend."

# *I'm Nervous to Make the First Move*

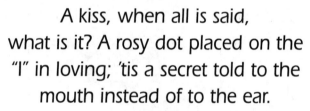

A kiss, when all is said,
what is it? A rosy dot placed on the
"I" in loving; 'tis a secret told to the
mouth instead of to the ear.

Edmond Rostand

*Dear Kim,*

*Sometimes I hate being a guy. We are always the one who is expected to ask girls out, call them on the phone and make the first move.*

*I have a girlfriend and I know she is waiting for me to kiss her. I want to kiss her, but I am really scared. Why do we always have to be the ones to initiate everything?*

Well, I am sure you know it used to be much worse. There was a time when a girl could not call a guy no matter what. And be the first to kiss him . . . forget it.

You are right, though; even though things have changed, most of the responsibility is still put on the guy.

So . . . you could be creative and say something like, "If you want to kiss me, feel free to any time now." Or, "I am just waiting for you to make the first move." You could do that, or you could just kiss her. As I am sure you already know, it will be very easy—one of the easiest things you have ever done. The scariest part is what you are going through right now: the anticipation. So the faster you just go for it, the sooner you can begin to enjoy it. (She is just as nervous, trust me.)

# I Don't Get It: What Is Love?

♥

Love is not what we become,
but what we already are.

Stephen Levine

*Dear Kim,*

*Everyone is talking about love all of a sudden. My friends who I used to go shopping with, hang out with and share everything with are all talking about how they are in love with this guy or that guy, and it's driving me crazy.*

*I am feeling kind of stupid because not only have I not been in love, I seem to be very confused about what it is. How can someone love someone more than anything one day and hate that person the next? Sometimes, it is even the other way around, which makes even less sense. Whenever I ask my friends to explain to me what this love thing is all about they just laugh and say, "You'll see." Can you please explain?*

Good question. First, let me say that philosophers and poets have been trying to answer that question since the beginning of time, so you certainly shouldn't feel stupid that you don't have all the answers. In fact, you pose some very good questions.

You needn't worry, for I am sure you will understand your friend's feelings sooner or later. I've come up with a few ways to identify love specifically for teenagers. I invite you to send in additional definitions for a next book or a Web page posting.

**Love is . . .**

. . . when you feel something more than friendship but can't quite describe it.

. . . when you begin to see someone in a very positive light.

. . . suddenly being nervous, shy and unable to think of anything to say whenever you are near a certain someone.

. . . wanting to be close to someone, both emotionally and physically.

. . . being excited about going to school because you know you are going to see him or her.

. . . wanting to look your very best when you know you will be seeing him or her.

. . . caring for this other person in ways you haven't cared before.

. . . not hearing a word your science teacher said because you spent the entire class thinking about, or, better yet, staring at, him or her.

. . . wanting nothing more than to see that person smile.

. . . growing faint when that person smiles at you.

. . . not caring if your friends don't think he/she is the cutest guy/girl in the world, because you do.

. . . being willing to stick around and work things out when difficulties start arising.

. . . rushing home to call or be called by him or her.

. . . being able to be smart and fun around everybody until he/she shows up and then you are unable to say anything that even makes sense.

. . . listening to the words to songs that you never bothered listening to before.

. . . wanting to read poetry in hopes it will express what it is that you are feeling.

. . . thinking that everything he/she does is so incredible. You've never met anyone so interesting, so funny or so cute!

# *Love Is Sweet*

### TIFFANY STORM

---

## Love is always present, it is just a matter of feeling it or not.

Kimberly Kirberger

---

Growing up in an enormous world lends itself to many firsts: first steps, first words, first solid foods. . . . And as the years pass, the firsts become more monumental and life-changing and less of a hushed "Aw . . ." from a mother or father. I know. It was one of those firsts that I am thinking about now.

As a sixteen-year-old full of unanswered questions, I sought the answer to love with an undying determination. I wanted to be part of it! I wanted to master it! But most of all, I just wanted to experience it.

Ben and I had been friends for as long as I could remember, from piggyback rides and colorful stories from a teacher in the second grade to an interest in poetry in the eighth grade. We saw life through the same eyes and questioned each other about it frequently.

In the eleventh grade, something had changed between Ben and me that I didn't understand. I received no more stuck-out tongues, but now wholehearted smiles. Less tugs and teases and more sideways glances and phone calls. I went from feeling small to suddenly feeling so important. Was this love?

Ben and I began seeing each other often, and, before long, I felt like a permanent fixture in his family. I didn't understand this time together or why things always seemed to work when we were together, but I enjoyed it. After one particular weekend of seeing each other Friday night, all day Saturday and Sunday afternoon, I looked at my friend and asked shyly, "Don't you ever get sick of me?"

Hanging in the air, my worst fear was now out in the open. A thousand "what ifs" ran screaming through my mind. I truly could not imagine how a person could enjoy my company as much as I enjoyed his.

"Do you ever get sick of the sunshine?" Ben answered sincerely.

Ben and I continued to spend much time together that year. The song "You Are My Sunshine" suddenly meant more to us than words could explain. The lyrics spelled out the true meaning of life to Ben and me: to love and be loved in return.

Ben and I have since parted ways, but I learned so much from him. Never again will I feel small and insignificant. We each carry our own little "sunshine," and it is our job to share it.

# Five

# Do You Like Me???

do you like me
do you like me
tell me if you do!
because if you like me
I'm quite certain
that I like you, too!

Kimberly Kirberger

"When a guy flosses his teeth with a strand
of your hair, does it mean he's really romantic, or does it
mean he's the most disgusting guy in school?"

# Do You Like Me?

♥

Courage is not the lack of fear.
It is acting in spite of it.

Mark Twain

How many times have we all wondered if someone liked us? Of course, there are those times when we wonder if a friend or someone we just met likes us, but I am talking about the big question: Does the person I like, like me back? Does that person find me attractive? Am I good enough? Is there a chance for us to be together? Does that person even know I exist? Am I liked as a friend . . . only? Do I have a chance? Is he or she available? If there's no special someone in that person's life, would he or she like me? The questions go on and on. Wouldn't it be incredible if we had some kind of magic ball that contained all the answers? Think of the time that would be saved if we did. Think of the embarrassment we would be spared, not to mention the heartache.

We *don't* have all the answers, though; and, truthfully,

this lack of information makes love all the more exciting. As for the heartache and embarrassment, we can do some things to ease the pain.

Some basics:

- Be sure that your feelings are yours and not someone else's.
- When you are sure of your feelings, don't be afraid to let the other person know.
- There is a difference between liking someone and wanting someone to like you.
- Just because someone else doesn't choose you to be his girlfriend or her boyfriend doesn't mean that something is wrong with you.
- Not everyone you like is going to like you in return.
- When someone likes you, and you don't like him or her, be gentle with that person's heart.
- Love is very confusing all by itself. Try to keep it as simple as you possibly can.
- If you like someone and that person doesn't like you back, do everything you need to do to get the hurt out of your system. Cry, talk to your best friend about it as much as you need to, and then move on.
- Rejection isn't personal. It isn't personal. It isn't personal. It isn't personal.
- Love works in mysterious ways.

# The Boy Next Door

BECCA WOOLF

## To love at all is to be vulnerable.

C. S. Lewis

I moved in when I was seven years old, and even as a gangly seven-year-old, I had eyes for the boy next door.

We grew up together. He taught me how to climb trees, how to skateboard and how to cuss.

Years passed and uncountable love notes were placed upon his doorstep. I remember waiting and waiting for replies; but, somehow, they must have been lost along the way, although my naïveté didn't let me care too much.

And then one day, I did care. It's funny how the changing seasons can bring reality to a little girl in pigtails and cause her to see out of the eyes of a young woman. All of a sudden, I became overly sad when he ignored me, and overly happy when he smiled at me. I scribbled his name all over my folder and read it with lovesick eyes. "B. Jay," it said. "I love B. Jay."

Unfortunately, by the time I was in seventh grade, he was way out of my league, and, worst of all, he knew it. I would stare at him from across the hall, and, when his eyes met mine, he would quickly look away, pretending not to see me. I guess I wasn't pretty enough or cool enough for his attention, and I wondered how he had so easily forgotten the days when we would run away from the world and hide for hours in the tree fort we built together out of plywood and old sheets.

Then one day, as I was munching on my after-school snack, the phone rang, and it was him. B. Jay. I was confused. He had been avoiding me for months. Why would he just call out of the blue?

"Do you wanna, uhhh, come over?" His voice was unfamiliar. It took me no longer than a second to reply.

"Okay. Sure, yeah, sure, umm, yeah," I stuttered nervously.

Dial tone.

I was too excited to realize he hung up without saying good-bye. I walked quickly and casually to his front door, reminding myself to be cool.

The door opened, and I walked inside. His house smelled like old leather and detergent. I breathed it in nervously.

"My parents aren't here," he said smiling.

I smiled back, completely unaware of what he meant.

He plopped down on the couch and turned on the TV.

"Sit down," he said with the same silly grin.

So I sat . . . and we stared at the TV. . . . And then it happened. Don't ask me how. I was too busy wondering how to act, but there he was leaning in to . . . yes to . . . kiss me.

My heart stopped. I swear it must have, because I lost feeling in my body and I couldn't breathe. I must have looked somewhat awkward because I had absolutely no idea what I was doing, and my plan to act "cool" turned into my pretending I was a complete expert.

But I didn't care; my dream was coming true. We were together at last . . . and forever. . . . Life was pure perfection.

And then the kiss was over, ending as awkwardly as it began. We both returned to staring at the TV. I was eager to run home and tell my friends, so I kissed him good-bye and sprinted home.

The next day at school, I saw him in the halls.

"Hi, B. Jay," I exclaimed.

He didn't say a thing. He just walked by as if I didn't even exist.

"B. Jay, B. Jay . . ." The louder I called his name, the faster he walked away.

I was completely horrified. What happened? I thought we were going to be together forever, I thought he loved me or at least liked me.

I went home sick that day.

It was many weeks before I could face him again. I would lie in my bed, listening to guitar solos that rose from his garage, and cry. I waited for some sort of explanation or apology. But I knew one would never come; it was time to move on. And eventually I did. As the years passed, I have strengthened because of new heartaches and pain. I have learned neither to love nor to hate the boy next door, but, rather, to thank him for helping the little girl inside me to grow up.

"Being able to belch out 'Wild Thing' is something
that impresses guys, Bubba, not girls."

*Reprinted by permission of Dave Carpenter.*

# *What Do Guys Like?*
# *What Do Girls Like?*

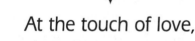

At the touch of love,
everyone becomes a poet.

Plato

*Dear Kim,*

*I am so depressed. No matter what I do I cannot get a boyfriend. I know this sounds weird, but for some reason, guys just don't like me.*

*What am I doing wrong?*

There is, of course, no way I could know why you are having this problem. What I will do, though, is make a list for guys and for girls of ways to attract the opposite sex. I may say some things over and over in this book but don't worry; they are all things that are worth repeating.

## What Guys Like

- Guys like girls who take good care of themselves. This isn't about model beauty. This is about clean hair, smelling good, exercising. By taking care of yourself, you send out the message that you care about yourself. Guys like this!
- Guys like girls who have a life. They like it when you aren't always available. They like to know that if they like you, you aren't going to be needing them all the time.
- Guys like girls who have a sense of humor. This is one of the most underestimated attributes. Let's face it, we all love someone who laughs (especially at our jokes) and knows how to have fun.
- Guys like girls who don't try too hard. Once again, the message you send when you try too hard is that you are desperate. They want to think that they lucked out by getting you.
- Guys like girls who listen to them and find them interesting. Don't fake it, but don't try to "get" a guy if you don't think he is interesting.
- Guys like girls who have fun with their girlfriends. They want to know that if they are going to watch the game on Saturday night, you aren't going to fall apart. They like girls who can have a good time *without* them.

- Guys like girls who sincerely like them. So . . . instead of thinking, "I want a boyfriend," think, "I am looking forward to meeting a guy I like who likes me back."

# What Girls Like

- Girls like guys who adore them. This is the number-one thing for girls. Many a girl has fallen in love with a guy after he announces that he likes her. The more you like her, the better (unless it is overbearing).
- Girls like guys who are strong. They like guys who are confident and give them the feeling that they are safe when they are around them.
- Girls like guys who aren't afraid to say sweet things to them. "You look so pretty tonight." Stuff like that.
- Girls like guys who don't shy away from them when their buddies are around.
- Girls like guys who know how to have fun when they are with a girl (besides being physical).
- Girls like guys who make them feel special.
- Girls like guys who care about their feelings and who aren't afraid to talk about "emotional" stuff.
- Girls like guys who are thoughtful, who call just to say "hi," "good night," or to see how they are doing.
- Girls like guys who are generous. Not just with money but in other ways, too. They like guys who will go out of their way to make them feel comfortable.
- Girls like guys who take care of themselves. They like clean hair, nice clothes, and they love a guy who smells good.

- Girls like guys who do little things like hold their hand softly, move their hair away from their face for them or remember the day they first kissed.

# *Illusion*

## JULIAN ARIZONA

I thought I saw you look at me,
I thought I saw you stare.
Do you know I think you're cute?
I like the look you bare.
Are my eyes deceiving me,
when I see you standing there?
Are you playing tricks on me,
just to prove I care?

Are you an illusion,
is it only in my mind?
Do you look at me,
as I do you,
to see if you can find
a little bit of interest,
a stolen glance your way?
Will you come and talk to me,
or watch me day to day?

You may have taken notice
that I'm not very shy.
I like to tell my girlfriends
when I like a certain guy.
I do not mean to scare you,
but I've thought of you a lot.
and now I simply want to know,
do you like me, too—or not?

"We'd like everything to be as romantic as possible.
On our pizza, can you arrange the anchovies into couples?"

# I Freeze When I'm Around Her

## We can only learn to love by loving.

Iris Murdoch

*Dear Kim,*

*There is a girl who goes to my school, and I like her . . . a lot. I have had a crush on her for a long time, but I can't even talk to her. Whenever I am around her I freeze. I just can't talk. It is so weird. I am fine around other girls; in fact there are lots of girls who like me. But whenever I am around her, I turn into an idiot. I am sure she thinks I hate her because I never even say "hi" to her.*

*What should I do?*

Well, I think everyone has had this experience. Girls and guys get shy when they are around the person on whom they have a crush.

The best advice I can give is try not to think about it. The next time you are around her, force yourself to say something . . . even if it is just "hello." You can begin by saying "hi," or even by just nodding in response to something she said. If other people are around, talk to them, but look at her while you are talking. The more you can do these small things, the more comfortable you will be, and, soon, you'll be your charming self. Remember, the longer you wait to do something, the worse it becomes. You will only be more nervous each time. These things won't go away without some effort on your part.

"Now that I've quit hating girls, I've got pimples."

# How Can I Tell If He Likes Me?

*Dear Kim,*

*How can you tell if a guy likes you?*

When we develop a crush on someone, our heart starts beating faster, blood rushes to our face and everything becomes intense. It would be great if we could just approach the person we like and say, "Hi, I find myself thinking about you a lot lately. Would you like to go out with me?" It just doesn't work like this, though.

First let me say that the answers I am going to give you are not foolproof. For instance, if I say, "When you find that he stares at you all the time," this doesn't always mean he likes you. It is just one example of something guys do when they like you.

So, here are some ways you can tell if a guy likes you:

- He stares at you a lot.
- He smiles at you when he sees you.
- He flirts with you.
- He talks to everyone around you but never directly to you, although he is probably paying attention to your reaction to his jokes, etc.
- He makes sure he is included in group plans of which you are a part.
- He attends parties that he knows or thinks you will be attending also.
- His voice gets lower when he is around you.
- He calls you just to talk.
- He gets friendly with your best friend.
- He starts combing his hair and wearing nicer clothes. (This means he likes *somebody*.)
- He asks your friends about your plans. "Is Sue going to the party?"
- He asks your friend if you have a boyfriend.
- He just shows up and walks with you to class.
- He starts e-mailing or instant-messaging you.
- Then one night, he calls and asks you to go out— and then, you can be pretty sure he likes you.

"If you really loved me, you'd send me romantic little
e-mails all day. That's what boyfriends do."

# How Can I Tell If She Likes Me?

*Dear Kim,*

*How can you tell if a girl likes you?*

Once again these answers are not foolproof, but some things to look out for are:

- She smiles at you all the time.
- She can't even look at you when you are close by.
- She giggles a lot in your presence.
- When you are with a group of people, she makes weird looks and facial expressions to her girlfriend whenever you do or say something.
- After you walk away, you hear one of them scream, "Ahhhhhhhhhh, he is so fine!"
- She is nice to your friends.
- Her best friend calls you and asks you questions

about her like, "What do you think of Susie?" Be forewarned: Susie is probably listening on the other phone.

- She sends you instant messages a lot.
- She just happens to be in places that you frequent, and you haven't seen her there before.
- If you play sports, she is at all your games.
- Look closely at her notebook for your name or initials inside of a heart.
- She flirts with other guys when you are around.
- She seems to be ignoring you.
- She has her girlfriend tell you she likes you—and then, you can be pretty sure she likes you.

# We Make Out . . . and Then It's Over

*Dear Kim,*

*I have the worst luck when it comes to guys. I have wanted a boyfriend for a long time now, but it never works out.*

*Every time I like a guy, the same thing happens. He will ask me out or we will hang out at a party, but then he disappears. The thing that bothers me the most is I feel like all they want is to make out with me and then once we do they dump me. What should I do?*

All of us want to be loved, and we all have times when we feel like we would do anything to get that love. The problem is, we can't make another person love us, no matter how hard we try.

Let me back up a little here. You meet a guy at a party, and you like him. It sounds to me like the next thing you do is make out with him. Although it is easy for something like this to happen, I think this could be the problem.

Guys like the chase. They will often try to kiss and make out as soon as possible, but this is not the best way "to get" a guy. Even though it sounds like "adult advice," and you are probably thinking that all adults say that, it is true.

What's the hurry? When you meet a guy, it is fine to let him know you are interested. It is fine to flirt with him and make plans with him for the next day or weekend. But if you want him to stick around, don't hook up with him right away.

Sometimes we think, "If we kiss then it will be official. Not so. This is a "girl thing." Guys *don't* think that way. They don't feel obligated simply because they kissed you. Trust me on this one—no need to rush.

# Sweet Dreams

KELLY GARNETT

---

## If I know what love is,
## it is because of you.

Herman Hesse

---

Looking back on it, I am surprised that I made it through elementary school . . . that I passed through junior high with decent grades, and that I even eventually graduated and got my diploma. Because while everyone else was studying English, math and science, I was studying Aaron.

He became my favorite subject right from the very first day we met. He had more freckles then, and fewer teeth (we were six), but I knew instantly that there was no one else for me. And from the beginning on the playground, there grew a constant and unchanged relationship between him and me. I adored him—and he made fun of me.

We seemed to always be thrown into each other's paths as the years went on, so there was never a time when he was not part of my life. And as we grew older, we grew to be better friends. Though he seemed to live to torment me, he also seemed to respect my advice, and he would ask for it in occasional frantic phone calls.

I knew everything about him. I paid so much attention to Aaron that I think I knew him better than he knew himself. I watched as he became everything that I had always known he would—a leader in student government, a star athlete and homecoming king.

I led the more typical life, with many friends, but not in the most popular circle of people—with school activities like the choir instead of cheerleading. And I had other guys who caught my attention. I had relationships with boys I cared about very much and crushes on guys I knew I would never even talk to. But it all made little difference whenever Aaron found a minute to smile and say "Hi" in the hallway—my stomach knew him well and always did the old flip-flop.

He was the only one I had ever known who had the power to affect me so deeply. He could ignore me one day, sending me home with scores of bad poetry in my diary, and give me a compliment the next that left me on cloud nine for the rest of the week. It was a kind of torture that, given the chance, I would have never changed, because it felt so wonderful to feel something so deep in my heart.

Inside, I always knew that he would never feel about me the way I felt about him. He and I lived in different worlds, and while he was a large part of mine, I was someone who was there to make him laugh, someone for him to tease . . . soon to be relegated to the background of his life. I expended a great deal of energy to ensure my spot in his life because I always regarded it as the most important thing, something I desperately needed.

I was amazed when he and I stayed friends after he went to a different school. He was always insanely busy, but found time to write once in a while. I even got him to agree to go out to dinner, after not seeing him in over a year; I got ready that night with butterflies in my stomach and the familiar rapid beating of my heart.

While later in the evening, sitting across the table from him, all alone, with his complete attention . . . I felt nothing. Somewhere, something had changed in me. The feelings I had experienced for almost an entire lifetime were replaced by feelings of contentment and the comfort one finds in old friendship. I was finally over him.

It felt odd at first, as though a piece of me were missing. After I left him that night, I spent a long time lying in bed and thinking of him, as I had done countless times before. I remembered time after time of smiling at the thought of him, and realized how lucky I was to have had a first love. It was a kind of love that was unique, and, no matter how many other relationships I had, one that would always be special . . . and I smiled one more smile for him as I fell asleep.

# Someone Special

OLIVIA ODOM

There's someone special in my life
Who doesn't know I care
I wish I could let him know it
But let it show, I wouldn't dare.

I don't want to even risk it
I don't want to even try
For if he knew I felt this way
I'd feel insecure and shy.

I never thought I'd feel this way
I never thought I'd care
There's something in that smile of his
That makes me stop and stare.

How can I tell if he likes me?
Will he ever look my way?
I'll keep my feelings hidden for now
And save them for another day.

*Six*

# When Friends Become More . . .

*Fate keeps on happening.*

Anita Loos

# *When Friends Become More . . .*

## Friendship is a single soul living in two bodies.

Aristotle

Falling in love with your best friend or your best friend falling in love with you is a very common scenario.

It isn't surprising that you would fall in love with a friend. After all, that friend is already someone you like and with whom you feel comfortable. It is often someone you already spend a great deal of time with and someone with whom you have spent thousands of hours on the telephone. You know this person's likes and dislikes, concerns and deepest insecurities. And, this person knows yours.

*So, what is the problem?*

Well, first of all, these feelings are not always mutual.

The friend may want to remain just that—a friend. There is also the discomfort that occurs when the other person knows you feel "differently." Oftentimes he or she feels guilty or maybe even threatened. Whatever it is that the other is feeling, it can become very complicated.

Once again, honesty is always the best policy. Even if it seems like being honest will mess things up, possibly even destroy a perfectly good friendship, it is always the best way to go. In the long run, you won't regret it.

I know of many times when friends have become girlfriend and boyfriend, and everyone ended up happy. But, even when the relationship thing doesn't work out, with honesty, the friendship can survive and even become stronger.

So . . . if you like your friend as more than a friend, hang in there. Don't ever give up hope. Things will work out . . . one way or another.

# My Best Friend

## SAMANTHA JOSEPH

---

For those passionately in love, the whole world seems to smile.

David Myers

---

He looked at me. His eyes, they sort of smiled. I guess it was right then that I realized I had loved him all along. "You know what?" he said. "You are my best friend, Jessi." He told me that I was his best friend. *But, I love you*, I wanted to say. *I don't want to be just your best friend.* Of course, I told him none of that. I just smiled and said, "And you're mine." But that's not all, that's not enough, my heart was about to burst. What was I going to do? I guess I had to make a choice. I could be his best friend or nothing at all. He didn't love me, not like that. So, I smiled again, walked into my house and closed the door. I was okay, I was. At least, I wanted to be. I really did, but I just couldn't seem to stop the tears streaming down my cheeks. I wasn't okay. Ten minutes later the phone rang. It was Marc, of course. "I told you that you were my best friend, right?" he asked, jokingly. I managed a laugh and told him to go do his homework. He was my best friend.

*How could I have told her that she was my best friend? I thought that the minute I said it. What's wrong with me? I had to call her afterwards, just to make sure that I actually had. I couldn't believe it. I love you, Jessi; I'm in love with you. That's what I meant to say. I don't want her to be my best friend; I want her to be my, well, everything. She is everything. Now what do I do? Stupid, Marc, very stupid. Now, she's your best friend.*

It's been a while now since Marc told me that he wanted me to be his best friend. I think that I need to move on. He and I would never work anyway. At least, that's what I've been telling myself. I think my head is close to believing me, but my heart just can't. No, there's nothing I can do, and I have to move on. I'll be exactly what he wants me to be; I'll be his best friend.

*Jessi called me up today. It's been a whole week since I said the best-friend thing. She's been great, but, well, she's been my best friend. Anyway, she called to tell me about this guy from school, Dave. That was awkward. The harder I try to let go of her, to stop, you know, loving her, the more I can't. It's not fair, and hearing about other boys doesn't help. But, that's what best friends do, right? They talk about other people and who they like. I guess she believed me about before. Why did she pick now, of all times, to believe me? Why is she only my best friend?*

This guy, Dave, asked me out in school today. He seems

nice enough, but he's not . . . he's not Marc. I wish I didn't feel this way, I wish I could help it, but no such luck. I called Marc after it happened to talk to him about it. It was hard, but I figured it was the first step to being his best friend. I mean, best friends talk about that sort of thing. It was weird though; he was weird. It was almost like he didn't want to talk to me about it. I just can't seem to figure him out lately. I hope everything's okay, that we're okay. I hope that I can at least be his best friend.

*Jessi and I haven't been connecting lately. It's my fault; I've been pretty distant. I don't think she's noticed yet, though. She hasn't said anything. The truth is, this whole Dave thing is bothering me a lot more than I've let on to her. I don't want to be the one she talks to about boys; I want to be the one she talks about. I know that I blew it, but that doesn't change how I feel. I'm going to tell her. I have to. "Hello, is Jessi there?" I asked her mother on the phone. "Oh, she's out with Dave. Yes, thank you." Dave, huh? It's too late. I'm too late. She can only be my best friend.*

I had a date today with Dave. I guess it went okay. I mean, it was, but I couldn't stop thinking about, you know, Marc. I know he wants me to be his best friend, but I can't anymore; I never really could. I'm going to tell him, tonight. I just wish I could be sure that he can still be my best friend after I do.

*Maybe it's not too late. It was just one date, right? What could have happened in just one date? I'll talk to her tonight, when she gets home. I think that's the right thing to do. That is, of course, only if she still wants to be my best friend after I do.*

"I don't want you to be my best friend anymore," Marc told me. I was shocked. He told me that he needed to talk, but I never thought. . . . Why would he say that? What had I done that had made him so mad? Why couldn't I be his best friend?

*She cried after I said that, when I told her that she couldn't be my best friend. I didn't mean to make her cry, it just came out wrong. I raised my hand to her face, and I brushed away her tears. I looked at her, and I couldn't help it, I started to cry, too. "I love you and that's why. I just can't be your best friend anymore."*

I think he just told me that he loved me, but I'm not sure. Maybe I heard him wrong. This was Marc, the boy I had grown up with, the one who had very recently told me that he only wanted to be my best friend. "I love you," Marc said again. No, I was right. I was right! "I love you, too." That was all that I could say. I wanted to tell him that I always had, that I always would. I wanted to tell him how happy I was, how happy he'd made me. But, I just smiled instead, and I think he knew. After all, he's still my best friend.

*She said it back; she really did. Of all the things that I thought would happen, I hadn't prepared myself for this. I wanted to tell her again and again, how happy I was and how I loved her so much. I couldn't. Looking at her, with that smile on her face . . . she left me speechless. You know what, I think she knew anyway. I must be the luckiest person in the whole world. Not only does she love me, but she's also my best friend.*

# Help . . . I Have a Raging Crush on My Best Friend!

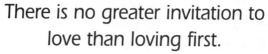

There is no greater invitation to love than loving first.

St. Augustine

Dear Kim,

I never thought it would happen to me. I used to watch my friends giggle and act stupid over some guy and I would think to myself, "No way! Not me!" I honestly believed I would never "like" a guy or be involved in any of those ridiculous dramas that I have so often watched my friends engage in. Well, I was wrong on both accounts. Not only am I absolutely, madly in love with a guy named Ryan, but I am smack in the middle of a drama that could teach Dawson and Joey the true meaning of the word.

*I have been laughing at his jokes and his antics for three years. Two years ago we called each other* friend, *and we even hung out together. I would go to his house and play video games or he would come to mine and swim with me in our pool. People would try to make stupid jokes, but to us that is what they were. What was their problem; can't a guy and a girl just be friends? Well, they can. It's just that until recently I never noticed how cute he was or how his eyes danced when he knew he had said something truly funny. I didn't notice the way he dressed, or the way he walked. Not until now. He is not plain and simple. He is funny and he is cute and he is making me crazy.*

*He is also clueless. He said something to my girlfriend the other day like, "Why is Jenn acting so weird?" She covered for me and said something highly intelligent and well thought-out like, "I don't know what you're talking about." Hopefully, he didn't notice when she ran over to where I was standing to tell me what he had just said. Hopefully he didn't hear me when I let out a rather large scream while jumping up and down and saying, "Tell me everything he said . . . right now! How exactly did he say it? When he said* weird, *did he say 'weird' or* weird?" *I'm sure she wished she had kept her mouth shut to begin with.*

*Anyway, my question is this: What should I do? What did he mean by "weird"? How do I act around him now? I am really confused.*

It is strange, isn't it, how one day everything is normal and the next day you are madly in love with someone you have known for years. You are by no means the first person this has happened to.

The good news is you guys have been friends. Because of that, you can be pretty sure that he likes you. Some questions you might want to answer are:

- Has he ever had a girlfriend?
- Does he have one now?
- What kind of interaction have you had with him lately?
- What is he referring to when he says you have been weird? Have you been nervous around him?

These answers will be helpful to you. Hopefully, he doesn't have a girlfriend and he is ready for these kinds of feelings. (Remember people mature at different times, and often girls mature faster than boys do.)

This is my advice: The next time you see him, flirt with him. Let him know that you think he is funny, cute and all the things you mentioned. Be subtle, but don't be so subtle that you come off weird. Smile at him, make an effort to talk to him or walk with him to class.

The number-one rule, in my opinion, is when you like someone, let that person know. Don't push yourself on the other person and don't do anything to make him uncomfortable, but certainly don't keep it a secret. Guys love to find out that someone likes them.

Although I know it is customary for messages to be delivered via friends—like so-and-so tells so-and-so that so-and-so likes him or her—I think it is a very good idea to keep this at a minimum. I think it would be ideal not to use this method of communication at all, although I do understand its advantages. The disadvantages should also be considered. First of all, you no longer have control over who knows this juicy tidbit of information. You therefore have no control over how this information is delivered to your crush. You also risk people talking and spreading untrue rumors . . . and you know the rest. It can get really messy before it even gets started. Who needs it?

My suggestion is, if you decide to share this information with someone, just tell your very best friend. Be very clear with her that she is the only one you are telling and that you want to keep it between the two of you. If you want her to tell Ryan, have her tell him directly. However, if you can be very brave, I suggest, when the time is right, you tell him. In the meantime, flirt, have fun and keep it between you and Ryan.

Most important, remember, this is your first crush. These feelings are new and can be very confusing. Take things slow, expect to be nervous and a bit dramatic, but don't beat yourself up for it. In fact, enjoy it. You will never have another first crush.

Whatever happens, you will look back on this someday and know that it was perfect. Try your best to keep that in mind now.

# The Key to My Heart

TAMMY OSBORNE

Late at night,
When I should be asleep,
Into my heart,
You quietly creep,
I sit and ponder,
How it could be,
But you must have stumbled,
Across the key,
I know our friendship,
Could mean so much more,
But it's up to you to open the door.

# The Day We Became More . . .

BRANDY NICHOLAS

Zack and I lay on our backs, staring at the ceiling. His hand rested lightly on mine, and we talked about where to go from this point. I was full of love for him as a friend, and I was so afraid to show more, even though he knew. He liked me, too, and after so many years of friendship, it was hard to go to the next level.

We both knew what we wanted but were uncomfortable making it happen.

Zack said to me, "I want to be with you."

I said the same.

And then he told me, "I don't know what to do. My mind is telling me one thing and my heart another."

I turned to him, the first time we had made eye contact in an hour, and I said to him, "Think with your heart instead of your mind. You think too much with your head. Your heart will show you the way."

That was when he leaned over and kissed me for the first time.

And he smiled and said, "Now I am thinking with my heart."

# I've Fallen for My Friend

♥

## And the trouble is, if you don't risk anything, you risk even more.

Erica Jong

*Dear Kim,*

*I have a friend in my youth group whom I have known for three years. One day I started thinking about him in a different way. In a love way. The next time I saw him, I couldn't even look at him, let alone have a conversation with him.*

*What I don't understand is: How is it that I was able to talk with him and be smart and funny a couple of days ago, and now I feel absolutely shy and insecure around him? All that changed was that I decided I had feelings for him. I know he is going to think I am really stupid if I keep acting like this. What can I do?*

This is a very good question and it has happened to, or will happen to, everybody at some point. When we are friends with someone, we enjoy that person's company, we care about our friend and we feel comfortable with him or her. Once we have "love feelings," more is at stake. Although a friend can hurt us, someone we are in love with can hurt us more. We become attached to that person and how he or she feels about us. We care much more about the way that person treats us, thinks about us and responds to us. Whenever we become attached to someone, we seem to lose a part of ourselves. Imagine that we all have a power center. From that center comes our personal strength, our security and our well-being. When we get attached to someone, and this is almost always the case when we have "feelings," we give away part of our power center.

This is why we hear expressions like *knocked off my feet, dizzy in love,* etc. This is why you are having trouble being secure in yourself.

I think it is best to be honest in all situations, including this one. So, first of all, tell him. Say something like, "You know I am feeling funny around you because I am beginning to like you as more than a friend." (He will be flattered.) Continue by saying, "Help me out here, are you having similar feelings or have I lost my mind?" He can then say either, "I am feeling the same way" or he can say, "You are losing your mind." This gives him a lighthearted way out, and it does the same for you, too. You can say, "Yeah, I thought so," and "Thanks for setting me straight." If this happened it would be easy for the friendship to stay intact; of course, if he answers the other way, you begin the delightful process of a relationship.

To give you a much simpler answer: Once you begin to develop feelings for someone, and therefore begin acting insecure and shy, it is always best to cut to the chase. The longer you let it build up, the more awkward it will become. It will not get easier, so you might as well go for it.

# With Honor

### ERIN KELLY

If I have to be your best friend
If that's all that I can get
Then I'll take the job with honor
I'll be the best one yet.
I'll offer you my shoulder
I'll show how I care
I'll be there when you need me
I'm not going anywhere.
If I have to be your best friend
The one who hears you cry
Then I'll take the job with honor
I'll take the job with pride.
My love for you is stronger
Than you will ever know
But for you to ever love me
I will have to let you go.
You need time to find your purpose
You need time to sort your thoughts
But when the course has ended
And the race is finally run.
Remember it's your best friend
Who has loved you from day one.

# I Want Him to Be My Boyfriend . . . Not Just a Friend

---

♥

---

Better to have loved and lost than
not to have loved at all.

Seneca

---

*Dear Kim,*

*James and I have been friends forever. When we first started hanging out, it was just a friend thing. It was cool having a guy for a friend because he would fill me in on the gossip, and I felt like I had inside info about guys.*

*About a year ago, I started falling in love with him. I didn't tell him or anyone else for a long time. Finally, it just started to drive me crazy. I told his best friend, knowing he would tell James. At first, James pretended that he didn't know, which was pretty funny, because I knew he did. . . . I'm not stupid. Anyway, once that charade was over, we had "The Talk." He got all sappy and said he loved me . . .* but just as a friend.

*I have tried to be just friends with him, but I don't like it. I just wish he would give me a chance, but he won't. I don't know what to do because I don't want to lose the friendship.*

*This is so weird!*

I called a friend of mine who is in a similar situation and asked her for some advice. She said that you should try to move on. Perhaps even find another boyfriend. If you do fall in love with someone else, your friend may then realize he does have feelings for you.

I think that if someone says he isn't interested in a relationship, it is a good idea to try to move on. If remaining friends is too difficult right now, you can always take a break.

It is very important to take care of *yourself.* If a break would help you to move on, just explain to him that a little distance is what you need.

Guys like it when a girl has enough self-respect to take care of herself. Whatever it takes for you to begin letting go of him, I suggest you do it. You'll be okay; it will just take time.

"Heather just gave 'the four dreaded words,'
'Let's-Just-Be-Friends.'"

# *More Than Friends*

ANONYMOUS

Whatever our souls are made of,
his and mine are the same.

Emily Brontë

We didn't start out as friends. I liked her; she didn't want to go out with me.

She said, "Let's be friends."

I said, "Okay," and that is how it all began.

I think she knew I was still in love with her. I mean, did she really think I could stop loving her just because she said she didn't want to go out with me? But I played along and pretended like that was all we were, and so did she.

She liked the attention, I am sure. Even though she insisted she wasn't interested in me in "that way," whenever something didn't go her way she would show up at my house. When things were going well for her, I was the first person she told. On weekends, we hung out together, rented movies and talked until the sun came up. At times, it seemed like we were boyfriend and girlfriend.

One night, I decided I was going to try to kiss her. *What do I have to lose?* I reasoned with myself. *How about your friendship?* my rational side answered back. My heart won out, and I decided I was going to go for it.

I was a wreck all night, and she noticed. She kept asking me why I was acting so strange. My hands were sweating and I was unable to sit still, but I didn't think it was that obvious. I answered her by saying that she was the weird one, and she started tickling me. She was always touching me. Didn't she know that drove me crazy?

We were watching a movie, and I was acting like those nerds you see on TV. I tried moving in closer without her noticing, yawning and putting my arm around her. I was being a first-class geek. I kept telling myself to just kiss her already, and then I did. Just like that.

At first, she was surprised. She kept talking even though I had my lips pressed up against hers. But, she didn't push me away and she didn't tell me to stop. Pretty soon, she was kissing me back.

It was a great feeling, except I was too busy thinking to enjoy myself. Thoughts were running through my mind like, "What am I going to say when we stop? What does this mean? What if this ruins our friendship?"

I almost didn't hear her when she said, "I have been waiting for you to do that for a very long time."

I have yet to top that moment. It was the most wonderful feeling. We made out for a long time, and then I suggested we go for a walk. We talked about our feelings, and we decided we wanted to be together.

It has been three months since that night, and we are still together. We have had our fights and our problems, but generally we have a good relationship.

Sometimes, we'll be goofing off or doing homework together and she'll say, "Hey, what are you thinking about?" I just look at her and smile.

Someday, I will confess that I am thinking about what would have happened if I hadn't had the courage to kiss her that night.

# I Finally Got the Girl— Now What Do I Do?

♥

## Love is not something you feel. It's something you do.

David Wilkerson

*Dear Kim,*

*I am so confused. I have liked this girl, Jane, for a very long time, but she just wanted to be friends. So I have been her friend even though I never stopped loving her and wanting to be her boyfriend. Now she says she wants to go out with me. So I should be happy, right? Well, instead, I am confused. She is kind of acting different, and, all of a sudden, I feel like she expects things from me but I don't know what they are.*

*I do love her, but I need some advice.*

I understand why you are confused. You are asking yourself things like, *"Why does she like me now? What changed? What are her expectations of me? Does she expect me to be more than I have been? What if it doesn't work? What if we lose our friendship?"*

There is something very magical about a friend who likes you as more than a friend. It is exciting and special. Even though she was saying she just wanted to be friends, you can be sure that she was loving the fact that you felt more for her. So now she has decided she wants to check you out. Obviously she likes you. She has had a chance to get to know you as a friend, and she likes what she has seen. Perhaps she thought about how she would feel if you began to like someone else and realized that she would be upset. It's hard to know what motivated her decision to get more involved, but I think you are in a good position.

As for her acting weird, I am sure it feels strange for her to be having these new feelings for you. It will probably take a while for her to get used to them. If you think she is going to ask for too much from you, like too much time or too much attention, you just have to be clear and honest with her about what you feel comfortable with. If you aren't willing to give up the time you spend with your friends, then don't. Be nice about it but don't give in, because you will just end up resenting her. Be sure to take things slow, for both of your sakes. Just take things one step at a time. I think a relationship that starts out as a friendship has great potential.

Love is about taking risks. Considering what you have told me, I think this is one worth taking. Good luck!

# Are We Better Off Just Being Friends?

♥

We define love as a delight
in the presence of the other person
and an affirming of his value and
development as much
as one's own.

Rollo May

*Dear Kim,*

*Sometimes love and all that goes with it are so confusing and strange to me.*

*I am having a problem with my sometimes girlfriend (currently ex-girlfriend), and I am not even sure how to explain it. I think, to start with, we make better friends then we do girlfriend and boyfriend, but, we love each other, so it is hard to stay just friends.*

*I really like her and she likes me. When we are just friends, we have a blast together. We laugh and go out and talk about everything. When we are together as a couple, we fight and expect too much of each other.*

*She wants to get back together and give it one more try, but I really think we should just leave it. I am not sure how to tell her this because I don't want to hurt her, and, most of all, I don't want to ruin our friendship.*

I think that you should tell her that you just want to stay friends for now. It is what you want, and, whether we like it or not, the person who doesn't want a relationship is the one who gets his or her way.

It sounds like it is more a matter of not letting go than a matter of you guys belonging together. You tried a couple of times, and it didn't work. I think taking a break is just what is needed.

So often we end up in a relationship just because we couldn't let go and move on. It isn't a good reason to stay or get back into a relationship. Do the friend thing for now; that is the one that seems to work.

# My Friend Talked to My Crush and Ruined Everything

♥

One makes mistakes: That is life.
But it is never a mistake
to have loved.

Romain Rolland

Dear Kim,

*Drew and I were best friends. We hung out, talked on the phone every night and confided in each other. We were so close. Last year, I started to get a crush on him. I tried to ignore it and succeeded for a while. But then I was really falling in love with him. Everything he did was so awesome, and he just kept getting cuter and cuter. I told my girlfriend about my feelings for him and she told him. She was just trying to help because, she said, she was sure*

*he felt the same way. Well, now he won't even talk to me.*
*It has been almost a month since she told him, and he*
*never calls me and I never see him. I am so confused. It is*
*like he is mad or something. I am so hurt because I have*
*lost my friend just because I fell in love with him.*

Yikes!!! Maybe he is confused. Maybe he is scared
Maybe he is crazy. . . . I honestly don't know.

Guys tend to become very confused when something
like this happens. They know what they have with you
and now you want it to be different. I am sure he doesn't
hate you, like you fear. I am sure he is suffering as much
as you are. If I were you I would make him talk to me.
Pick a time when he will be mellow and alone. (*Never* try
to talk to a guy around other people.)

Convince him that no matter what he is feeling, he
will feel better if he talks about it. Assure him that you
can handle anything. (You can cry later.)

Tell him that the bottom line is that you two are
friends,and he can tell his friend (you) anything.

Tell him you just want to know what happened.

Tell him you still want a friendship with him and that
he doesn't need to be afraid of what you are feeling.

Most important, *listen* and ask him to please help you
understand.

I really hope this works. But, if he is still unwilling to
talk after all that you have said, then he probably isn't
emotionally mature enough for you, and it's time for you
to let go. Let's see what happens!

Linda told all of her deepest, most private secrets to her beloved Teddy Bear. Little did she know, Teddy blabbed his mouth off.

# Good-Bye

BECCA WOOLF

And so it comes just as it is
a day no longer here
and through my trembling fingertips
the memories of the year,
I wave farewell to all our dreams,
I will forget you never.
I wonder if our crazy times
will stay with you forever.
But as I cry in pain of losing
My dear and such good friend
I will not close the book and say,
"Farewell, this is the end."
For good-byes create swift hellos
And days from now you'll see,
That though it hurts to say good-bye,
Your friend I'll always be.

# I Like Her . . . but She Likes My Friend

Dear Kim,

*I have had a crush on this girl for a long time, but I have never had the nerve to tell her. I hang out with her a lot, but she thinks of us as friends. I kept telling myself that I would tell her how I felt the next time we were hanging out, but every time I would chicken out.*

*Well, the last time we were together, she told me she liked my friend, Paul. My heart just broke, and I couldn't even talk. She asked me if I would find out if he likes her. So, even though I didn't want to, I asked Paul what he thought of her. He said, "I don't know, why? Does she like me?" Then he goes on to say stuff that was not very respectful, like that he would be happy to go with her for other reasons than liking her. He said he'd be happy to use her.*

*The next day at school, I saw him flirting with her and she was so happy.*

*What do I do?*

This breaks *my* heart. I can't imagine how awful this must be for you. I would like to tell you that life is fair and you will eventually win the girl . . . but the truth is I don't know what will happen.

I think I would tell her what Paul said . . . very gently. *But* . . . that isn't necessarily what I am saying you should do. All scenarios could backfire. *But,* if you can be clear that the bottom line is that you want to be honest—not to hurt her, not to ruin her relationship, but just to be honest—then this is what I'd do.

Call her, make a plan to hang out.

Say to her, "Look, remember when you asked me to talk to Paul? Well, I did." And then gently tell her what he said.

Now one thing to consider (I just thought of it myself) is that maybe Paul was just acting all tough around you, and maybe he really does like her.

*Changed my mind . . . new plan!!!* This is a better plan. Talk to Paul. Don't attack or accuse, just say that you need him to know a couple of things. Tell him that you have feelings for Paula and that it hurts you to think he is just using her.

Or, just say it in whatever way feels right for you.

I think what is most important is that you don't play the martyr here.

Talk about it. Tell him how you feel. Then, if he continues to say disrespectful things about her, do what feels right—*tell her!*

Tell her how you feel; then at least you have put your cards on the table. As I said before, the most important thing is to not be a martyr. Take care of yourself and let the cards fall where they may.

Good luck. I always like to see the good guy win!!!!

# Identical Friends

JANE WATKINS

Here is a tale
of the trouble love sends,
To a pair of inseparable
very best friends.

These very best friends
had the same taste in boys,
Just like as tots when
they liked the same toys.

They never did struggle
to borrow or lend,
They knew that sharing
was being a friend.

One defending the other
when teased or called names,
One choosing the other
when teamed up for games.

They were experts at sharing
fears, sorrows, and joys,
And their bond was rock solid
till they cared about boys.

It turned out they always
liked the very same boy,
But this would be different
from sharing a toy.

Will their friendship survive
their concerns of the heart?
Or will their love for one guy
tear their friendship apart?

It is yet to be known
how this sad story ends,
For they must choose
between guys or best friends.

They can ditch all they have
for the love of one guy,
Or hold on to their friendship
and wave him good-bye.

*Seven*

# Unrequited
# Love

*To love and win is the best thing.*
*To love and lose, the next best.*

William M. Thackeray

# *Unrequited Love*

♥
───────────────────

True understanding is
deeper in meaning than in mere
words and is important for its result,
not pretty rhetoric. Those who can
verbalize their happiness have little
happiness to speak of. My true love
has grown so much that I can't tell
even half of it in words.

Juliet in *Romeo and Juliet* by William Shakespeare

───────────────────────────────────

Oh, how it hurts to love someone and be denied his or
her love in return. This is one of the most painful things
that you will ever experience, and yet I doubt there is
anyone who hasn't had to go through it at least once in
his or her life.

There was one big one for me, and I will never forget
how badly it hurt. I was so in love with this guy. At first

he was in love with me also. We had such a good time together, and when I was with him I never wanted anything else. Just being with him was enough. He understood me in a way I have never felt before, and he always knew what I was thinking or feeling. He cared about my feelings, also. I could go on and on here, but the point is that one day he was with me and the next day he was not. I just couldn't accept it. I felt that he loved me as much as I loved him and he was just scared.

I thought he would come back. He would see how much he loved me and that he had made a terrible mistake.

As time passed and he was happy with his new girlfriend, I had to accept that it was over. Which I did, but I still didn't let go. I dreamed about him at night and thought about him during the day. I couldn't understand how I could love him so much when he didn't love me back. It just didn't seem right. It felt like his heart would have to love me if I loved him. I would wonder if he ever thought about me. I would wonder if I ever meant anything to him. I would torture myself with these thoughts.

Slowly, he faded from my memory—never completely, but each day I thought of him less. Then I met someone whom I loved in a different way. It was calmer and sweeter. Somehow, I knew this man was my soul mate. He was the one I would love forever. Although I still think of my ex from time to time, the hurt is no longer there. As for my soul mate, he is the one with whom I will grow old.

I think the heart gets stronger when it goes through the experience of unrequited love. I believe that, because of this experience, my heart grew bigger, and, when I met the person I would spend the rest of my life with, I was able to love him in a way that I wasn't capable of before.

# Stupid Horse Jokes

### BRIANA HALPIN

No one has ever loved
anyone the way everyone
wants to be loved.

Mignon McLaughlin

I never dreamed I'd feel this way. I would never wait all afternoon by the telephone, would never feel that strange flutter inside my stomach when the abhorrent glowing piece of plastic began to shriek for attention. I would never lay awake at night for hours, playing his words and his laughter and his stupid horse jokes over and over again in my head. I would never put off my pre-calculus homework to sift through a red and blue shoebox filled with notes and birthday cards and drawings of deranged stick figures . . . all from the same person. And I would never, I mean *never,* shed a tear over any dumb boy. But I have. And I do.

It's a funny thing, love. I used to tell myself that if I ever started to fall into it, I would pull myself immediately out. I would throw it off of me in disgust, hurl it so violently that it would be reluctant to return. Love came so quickly, though, that I guess I missed my opportunity for defense. And the more I think about it, the less I *want* to defend myself. I want to hold on to my feelings, to clutch them around my shoulders like the fibers of a blanket. They keep me warm.

I used to think of sleep as a waste of precious time. There is, after all, an entire world out there to conquer. Now I detest the sound of my radio alarm clock—even when I *do* wake up to Pink Floyd—because waking up means that I'm alone again. My dreams are my only opportunity to be with him, to look into the darkness of his eyes and feel like more than just good old goofy Briana who fell chasing after the school bus in eighth grade: awkward with a talent for getting really bad haircuts, completely unglamorous but intellectually cultured, the girl who fainted in church three years ago and hasn't been back since, who won't stick a fork into anything that might have once been named "Bessie" or with the words "partially hydrogenated" on the label, who actually likes Latin, eats her vegetables, and uses words with more than three syllables, good old clumsy dependable buddy buddy buddy.

This thing inside of me is so strong that it seems as if it must be unique to me, and to my experience. It doesn't seem possible that anyone—including myself—could ever feel this way about anyone else. Reason tells me this is far from true. Innumerable throngs of artistic works—visual, literary and musical—have been devoted to the complex, intangible thing so simply represented by a flying baby with a bow, an arrow and a naked derriere. The entire history of this place we call our world has virtually been shaped by the presence—and sometimes the absence—of love. How many people have felt what I now feel? How many people have lived and died with the anguish of unrequited love? Because I think that's what I'm afraid of most. That I'll never know what the palms of his hands feel like against mine, that I'll never taste the sweetness of his mouth, that I'll never hear him speak my name in a prelude to anything but a stupid horse joke.

# The Letter
# I'll Never Send

REBECCA SCIDA

The letter I'll never send
Would calmly ask you why
You broke my heart in two
And told my love good-bye.

If I ever sent this letter
It would sweetly state
You tangled up your destiny
And interrupted fate.

The letter I will not write
Would casually inquire
How can you live without me—
I was your one desire.

If you received this letter
It would politely say
You need me in your life now
You can't go on this way.

The letter I'll never send
Would then be briskly signed
"Your one and only Love"
You know—the one you left behind.

# He Doesn't Know
# I Exist

*Dear Kim,*

*I like this guy and I don't think he knows I even exist.
What should I do?*

Well, the first thing you need to do is let him know you
exist.

- Do you ever talk to him?
- Is he in any classes with you?
- Do you have mutual friends?

Figure out a way to talk to him. If he is in any of your
classes, ask him about the homework. If you have mutual
friends, strike up a conversation about their plans.

Do something to let him know you like him. Flirt with
him or smile at him . . . something.

If it turns out he isn't interested, you will survive. I

think the fear of unrequited love is even worse than the reality, as long as you keep it simple to begin with. It is always more difficult to deal with someone not liking us if we have told everyone we know that we like that person. Then, for the next month, you find yourself having to answer everyone's questions about why it didn't work out, when you are trying to forget and move on.

So, to sum up:

1. Let him know you are interested.
2. Keep it between you and him or as few people as possible.
3. If he isn't interested, move on.
4. If he *is* interested, enjoy! (And be proud of your courage either way!)

# I Can't Forget Him

*Dear Kim,*

*I am having a very hard time getting over my first love. We were so perfect for each other. I will never understand what happened or how he was able to forget about me. We were very close, and he was very open with me about his life and everything. Then one day, out of the blue, he dumped me. He didn't do it in a very nice way either. He wrote me a letter, and it was kind of mean.*

*I haven't spoken to him since because he avoids me, and I am not going to chase after him. The thing is I keep waiting for him to change his mind and he hasn't. Everyone tells me to forget him and move on, but I can't help it. I think about him all the time. I dream about him at night. I wake up thinking about him in the morning. I know that my love for him is the real thing, and I know he loved me, too. Should I wait for him?*

I don't know the details but I have to wonder why you would want him back if he just dumped you without an explanation.

It is always difficult to forget your first love. In a way, you never will. I do think you should move on though. It doesn't mean you have to forget, and it doesn't mean that what you felt for him wasn't real. It just means you are taking care of yourself.

You may want to write him a letter and tell him how you feel and explain to him that you have *no* idea why he left you. There is always the chance that he is reacting to some rumor or some fear he has that isn't true. Even if that isn't the case, you will feel better if you say what you have to say. But once you have made this one last effort—that's it. Let it go!

# I'm Obsessing Big Time

*Dear Kim,*

*I am obsessing over this guy in my class. He is the finest, the most handsome, the most awesome creature I have ever seen.*

*I have always had pretty good luck when it comes to guys, but this is the first time I have ever felt like this about a guy. I am so nervous around him, and this just isn't like me.*

*I am usually very confident and even kind of arrogant around guys. That sounds bad, but what I mean is, I just never felt like this before and I don't know what to do. I am totally obsessed.*

Love is the great balancer. Love is the one thing that can make everyone humble at one time or another. Sounds like it is your turn.

Just because you feel this way does not, however, doom you to heartache. It is possible that you could be *really* lucky in love and win this one's heart, as well. It is also possible that it won't work out, and I guess we have to consider both possibilities.

If he ends up liking you and you go out, you will probably still feel some tension, but you will have fun and it will be quite a ride.

If it doesn't work out, you will probably obsess over him for a while. This is not good news, but it is the truth. I think we all have at least one person who we fall for in a big way, and even though we want him or her to love us more than anything in the world, it doesn't always work out that way. It takes a while to get over this. But you will. The good news is that it won't kill you; it will make you stronger and it will also make you kinder. The next time some guy is madly in love with you, you will find yourself being just a little kinder and a bit more compassionate.

I wish you the best, and I know that whatever happens, you will be a better person for it.

# No Matter What I Do, She'll Never Like Me Back

*Dear Kim,*

*I have been desperately in love with this girl for over a year now. No matter what I do, it just doesn't seem to work out and I am really going nuts.*

*She will call me and say she wants to go out with me and that she has liked me all along, but she couldn't break up with her ex or whatever. I'll get all excited, and, just when I think I am finally going to be happy, some other guy comes along and steals her away, or she gets scared and decides to stay home with her friends.*

*Sometimes I think she would like me better if I were mean to her or if I mistreated her, because those are the guys she ends up going out with.*

*Please tell me what to do.*

I am sure that many are reading this and realizing that they have a tendency to go out with the guy or the girl who treats them badly, the one who doesn't love them back. Everyone has this tendency but in different degrees. We all have a little something in us that thinks, "If that guy or girl wants me, there must be something wrong with him or her." There is a joke about not wanting to join any club that would have me as its member. The key here is to know that we can fall subject to these thoughts, but we don't have to—especially once we become aware of them. Of course, if this is what she is doing, there is nothing you can do to change her. You *can* change *yourself,* though.

It is possible that you are doing the same thing. After all, you've spent over a year going after someone who doesn't love you back.

Be patient. You never want to win someone by being mean or even playing games. Just be yourself, and if this seems to be an impossible feat . . . move on. Which, I must say, it seems like it is time to do. Who knows—there is probably a sweet and beautiful girl just waiting for you to get a clue. And, by the way, one of love's best jokes is that once you fall in love with someone else, guess who will come around. . . . You got it!

# He Doesn't Love Me Back

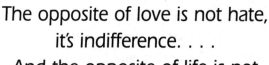

The opposite of love is not hate,
it's indifference. . . .
And the opposite of life is not
death, it's indifference.

Elie Wiesel

*Dear Kim,*

*I am so sad. I am in love with someone who does not love me back.*

*This is the most painful thing I have ever experienced. Please help me.*

Yes, it is very painful to love someone who does not return that love.

It is very hard to feel lovable when someone chooses not to love you back. Since I don't know the specifics of your situation, I can only say that as much as this feels like the end of the world, it isn't. And as much as it feels like a reflection on you and your worth, or lack of it, it isn't.

This is a time to be kind to yourself.

This is a time to be with friends who love you.

This is a time to write in your journal.

This is a time to make a list of all the things you like about yourself.

(This is a time to not think about what you don't like about yourself.)

This is a time to reflect and remember things change and this *will* pass.

This is a time to read a good book.

This is a time to say nice things to yourself.

This is a time to find the love you are looking for inside yourself.

# All I Can't Say

NINA YOCCO

There's so many words I can't say
when I look into your eyes.

Maybe you'll reject me
and shatter all my pride.

Each day my love grows stronger
but I won't let you know.

There's way too much behind my smile
that I can never show.

I'd hold you for a lifetime
if you would take my hand.

I'd love you like no other
but you don't understand.

Every time I see you
you're holding on to her.

The pain cuts like a dagger
making wounds that never cure.

So I'll dream of us together—
of how good it could be.

And I will keep the secret love
you could have had with me.

# I'm Waiting for Her to Decide

*Dear Kim,*

*I like this girl and I can't tell what she thinks about me. Sometimes she acts like she is interested, but most of the time she ignores me. I think she doesn't know how she feels and that is the problem. Any suggestions?*

Well, since I love simplicity, I have to vote for something easy and simple. *Ask her.*

I know things aren't always that easy, and I know she may not have a clue, but at least it gets things moving in the right direction, and it helps you to be in touch with your power.

I don't mean *power* the way it usually is used. I mean you are strong and you know what you want, and you will be okay no matter what she says or feels.

As long as you sit around wondering what she is thinking or feeling, you are giving her all the power.

Ask her, tell her how you feel, and then deal with whatever the outcome. At least you become the one in control of your life.

# Help . . . I'm Obsessing Over My Crush!

♥

What will not woman,
gentle woman dare; when strong
affection stirs her spirit up?

Robert Southey

*Dear Kim,*

*I am obsessed. I am in love with a guy at my school. He is a junior and I am a sophomore. I cannot think of anything but him, and it is starting to drive me crazy. I only see him for about five minutes total each day. The rest of the time I am either thinking about what I am going to say or what I said or what I didn't say or what I should have said. I am thinking about how he looks, how he talks and how he doesn't seem to know I exist. I think about how incredible it would be if he asked me out. This started out as a crush, and now it is taking over my life.*

*It isn't fun anymore, but I can't stop it. . . . I have tried, trust me. Please help me before I go insane.*

You are right, where you are isn't fun, and yes, it is crazy making.

Let's go back to the beginning. Try to remember the first time you "liked" him. Try to remember every detail of what really happened. It would be even better if you wrote all this down. Then try to go step by step and remember everything that has *happened*. The reason for this is that what often makes these crushes turn into obsessions is the imagination. So, the first step is to go over what has actually happened between the two of you.

Now try to look objectively at the events. Is there any chance for the two of you to get together, or is it basically hopeless? If there is a chance or if you strongly believe there is, then act on it *now*. Write a letter, send a message or talk to him directly. The reason this is so important is the more time you have to freak out about what to say or do, the crazier you will get about that. If he likes you, it is pretty much impossible to say or do the wrong thing right off the bat. If he doesn't like you, there isn't much in the way you approach him that is going to change his mind. If you feel there is no chance or if you have strong evidence to conclude that it "ain't happening," then it is time to do the following exercise.

The mind is a funny thing. The more you tell it not to do something, guess what it does? So telling yourself to stop thinking about him and "trying" to get over him probably won't work. In fact, it will make matters worse. So here is what you need to do: Invite one or two of your very best friends to spend the night. Tell them you need them to help you get over _____ once and for all. Explain to them that they will be doing you a favor and you are already grateful.

Gather together any pictures, notes or other memorabilia you have that has to do with him. Get all the heart-wrenching music you can find. (This exercise can also be done alone!) Get a box of tissues and a book of love poems. If you have written poetry or letters get them out also. Okay. Here is what we're going to do:

*Obsess.* (Remember, you warned your friends.)

Talk about him nonstop.

Play heart-wrenching music.

Act out your fantasy first date and continue on to the day you are married.

Completely, totally indulge in this crush.

Write letters and poems.

But, no matter what, do not under any circumstances think or talk about anything else.

Continue this *all night* or until you fall asleep.

Make an agreement with yourself to wake up the next day and tuck away all evidence of the previous night. You can either throw it away or store it in a box. But, without a struggle, just resign yourself to the fact that it is over for now, and you are going to move on. By letting yourself indulge and obsess, it will help you to get sick of it and get him out of your system.

A milder suggestion:

One thing that seems to work is to get involved with other things. Sign up for that art class you have been thinking about or make a movie date with your girl-friends. Try to keep busy. Just remember that you aren't "trying not to think about him," you are just doing other things.

When it comes to crushes, the more we try not to think about the person, the more we think about him or her. The more we promise ourselves that we are moving on, the more we remain stuck. This happens with other things in life as well: trying not to eat, trying not to laugh, and, my personal favorite, trying not to think about a monkey in the living room.

So, in closing, just keep in mind: "This, too, shall pass."

# She Loves Someone Else

*Dear Kim,*

*I just found out that the girl I like is going out with someone else. I shouldn't be surprised; she is so beautiful. I just feel like a jerk because I never told her or anyone else that I liked her. Now I will always wonder if she would have liked me or not.*

Well, the good news is these things usually don't last forever. It isn't like she got married.

This is one of those great experiences for learning. You will probably have another chance to tell her how you feel. If you don't and she stays with this guy for a long time, you may get a chance to tell someone else how you feel.

I was noticing something the other day about movies that ties into your question. Have you ever noticed how in scary movies the girl always goes down into the dark basement or attic with the lights *off?* Well, in romantic movies, the guy never tells the girl how he feels. I am always yelling at the screen, *tell her you love her!* (Sometimes it is the other way around, or in the really frustrating movies, neither one tells the other.)

If you think it is too late for this one, at least learn from this. One good way to build up "love-esteem" is to express your feelings. If you are interested in someone, let that person know. Once you are in a relationship, try to express what you're feeling. Each time you do, you will become a little bit more comfortable doing so.

Please know that none of us should ever be embarrassed about or ashamed of our feelings. If we can feel at ease with our feelings, then they won't have the same power over us. They will become like old friends, and each of us, in turn, will be comfortable in our own skin.

# I'm Obsessing Over Him

♥
_____

The story of a love is not important.
What is important is that one
is capable of love.

Helen Hayes

_____

Dear Kim,

Jake and I broke up over five months ago, and I still am not over him. I finally stopped talking about him to my friends because they got sick of it. My parents got sick of me moping around the house all the time, and my brother slams his door when he sees me coming now. I made everybody sick because I talked about Jake all the time.

I still love him, and I don't feel like it is getting easier. It is getting harder because each day that goes by, the memory of us together is harder to hold onto. I just feel like he is the only guy for me. I haven't even thought about anyone else; I don't want to.

I believe if Jake weren't so scared, he would admit that

*he feels the same way. He used to. We were perfect for each other. I can't change what I feel in my heart, and now I have to pretend that I don't feel what I do. I hate this.*

It sounds like you had something very special with Jake. That does make it harder to let go. The truth is, you don't *have* to forget about him. Your friends and your family are only trying to help. They would rather see you in love with someone who could love you back, someone with whom you could be happy, instead of a situation where you are miserable all the time. They may also be concerned that your feelings could be obsessive.

I felt the same way you are feeling at one time. What happened was, *he* left me, and I wasn't used to that. That, combined with the fact that I did love him very much, made me obsessive about him. I define *obsessive* as when we go on caring about, thinking about, talking about someone long after that person has moved on. Of course, this is normal to some degree, but when everyone you know is saying *enough,* chances are you have crossed over the line.

You are going through something we all experience at least once. I believe it is time to start reversing the direction of your energy by focusing on yourself—taking care of yourself, loving yourself and going easy on your heart.

Don't ask your heart to love someone who can't love you back.

*Eight*

# Now That We're Together

*Now join with your hands,
and with your hands
your hearts.*

William Shakespeare

# Now That We're Together

♥
_____

It was worth every minute.
The happiness and the pain were like
exercises for my heart, each time
leaving it in better shape
than before.

Kimberly Kirberger

_____

When you think about what it takes for two people to agree that they want to be together, it is a miracle that there is a thing called a relationship.

Many of your happiest memories will be those moments when the person you liked returned those feelings and you suddenly found yourself "involved" with someone. But like everything else in life, the fantasy is usually better than the reality, and with this new experience comes many new problems.

The best advice I can give you is to remember that relationships can bring you great happiness but also great pain. It all goes with the territory. But with all the heartache a relationship entails, it is still a wonderful and precious thing.

That is why the most famous relationship quote is one that reminds us, "It is better to have loved and lost than never to have loved at all."

I believe that one of our main goals as humans is to learn how to give and receive love. If we remember to always learn from what happens, then we will always be able to look at love and say, "It was worth every minute. The happiness and the pain were like exercises for my heart, each time leaving it in better shape than before."

Many times, you have heard people say a relationship takes commitment. This is often taken to mean that in order for it to work, you must promise to love the person forever and always. I think the kind of commitment that is needed is one that says:

*I am willing to learn from my mistakes.*
*I am willing to look at both sides of the situation.*
*I will communicate honestly and respectfully.*
And the big one . . .
*I will take responsibility for my part in this.*

Now I know this sounds very grown-up, but relationships are grown-up stuff. It is just that I happen to believe you guys are ready for this.

In this chapter, we will explore some of the situations

that happen once you are in a relationship. We couldn't possibly cover all the different scenarios, but we will cover the more common ones.

As for some general advice:

Enjoy the ride.

Listen to your heart.

Nobody is worth giving up your values for.

Friends will be around long after boyfriends or girlfriends.

You probably won't marry your first love.

You probably think you will.

As much as love hurts, it also heals.

Love yourself first.

Be kind to your own heart and to the hearts of others.

# Those Three Words!

## AMY ORTEGA

We'd been going out for three months before I told him that I loved him. It was late at night around one in the morning, and he had just left my friend's house where I was spending the night. My friend and I were up and were munching on junk food when I picked up the phone. His parents weren't home, so I dialed Brock's number. In a tired voice, he answered the phone. I simply said, "I love you," and then I hung up the phone. My friend Emily and I stayed up and laughed over my crazy way of telling Brock I loved him.

It wasn't until the following Monday that I saw Brock at school. Every day, he walked me to all my classes, but that day was extra special. When we stopped by the door of my first-hour class, Brock hugged me and whispered in my ear, "I love you, too."

# One Minute She's Nice, the Next She's Mean: What Am I Doing Wrong?

♥

It's terribly amusing how many different climates of feeling one can go through in a day.

Anne Morrow Lindbergh

---

*Dear Kim,*

*I don't understand girls at all. They say one thing and do another. They say they love you, and then they rip your heart out of your chest.*

*My girlfriend, or now ex-girlfriend, and I have broken up and gotten back together ten times. That should tell you something. She complains most of the time when we are together. I get sick of it and break up with her. I tell her, "If you are so unhappy, I think we should split."*

*She says fine and gets really mad and leaves or hangs up or whatever. She then makes a huge scene with her friends, my friends and anyone who will listen.*

*After some time has passed, she starts being sweet to me again. Sweet smiles, positive comments, laughs at my jokes. You know, the stuff guys like. Then I start to like her again. She can make me feel so great. She can make me feel like I am the best. Anyway, at this point, we get back together, and it is fun, great, perfect . . . for a while.*

*How can one girl make you feel so good and then so rotten?*

*What should I do? I miss her already, but I miss the good stuff, not the constant complaining.*

I love this question because it focuses on a very important message for making a relationship work.

When someone tells you that you are doing a "bad job" of loving him or her, it *does not* make you love him or her more. Let me put this another way. Being negative and complaining all the time is not the way to get someone to be nicer to you. You may be thinking to yourself, *How silly—of course it isn't.* But how many times have we all done this?

Relationships require positive input. People need to

hear what they are doing right. It does not work to tell others what they are doing wrong all the time . . . especially in relationships. Some of you may be thinking, "Well, that is really a bunch of bull. What if my boyfriend is messing up? Am I just supposed to let him? Or tell him he is doing a great job? I don't think so!"

I am not telling you to be deceitful. What I am saying is that complaining does not make the relationship better. Never has, never will!

If you think about it for a minute you will understand what I am saying. How could negativity make something—anything—*better?* Complaining to another person does not inspire him or her and make that person love you more. A relationship is not a "business deal." It isn't a situation where you can force another person to give you the love and admiration you want. We have to attract these things, not demand them.

In answer to your question, obviously there is something between the two of you, or you wouldn't have gone back so many times. Maybe it can be saved, maybe not.

For now, I would write her a letter. Tell her how much you love her. Tell her that when she is happy, you are, also. Explain that when she starts finding fault in everything you do, it disheartens you. As a result, you are unable to feel the love that you have for her. You could go on to say that you know you aren't perfect, but perhaps there is a better way to approach the problems that always come up for you guys. Try to discuss things with her when your relationship is going smoothly instead of waiting for the problems to occur and then trying to work them out.

Example: "I get my feelings hurt when you don't call me."

Instead of: "You don't call me enough."

Then you can do the same: "My heart closes when you criticize me."

Instead of: "All you ever do is complain."

If you guys can develop some good habits for discussing issues, then you have a chance of being able to hang in there when things get difficult.

Love is all about give and take, and I am not implying that this is all her fault by any means. You need to compromise and listen to what it is that is hurting her feelings. Then repeat back to her what you are hearing. "I hear you saying that it hurts your feelings when I don't call you. I will keep that in mind and make more of an effort. I sometimes feel like everything between us is based on rules instead of loving impulses. So I would be able to feel my love for you more if I didn't have so many rules about how to act. I want to just call you when I want to." Then you can go back and forth and discuss it until everything is out in the open. She might say, "Now that I understand your feelings, I only want you to call when you want to, unless we have plans that need to be discussed." These types of discussions can really strengthen a relationship, and they remove the negative attacks and hurt feelings.

I hope things work out for you guys and, if they don't, I hope I have been helpful to you for future relationships.

"I see your relationship with Linn is
still on-again/off-again."

*Reprinted by permission of Dave Carpenter.*

# My Boyfriend Treats Me Badly Around His Friends

♥
_____

The only love worthy of a
name is unconditional.

John Powell
_____

*Dear Kim,*

*I don't know what the deal is. My boyfriend is so nice to me when it is just the two of us. Whenever he is around other people, though—especially his friends—he treats me very badly. It is as if he is a different person. I understand the need for him to be cool and all, but his other friends are sweet to their girlfriends around him, so I don't get it.*

Is he mean to you or does he just kid around in a mean way? Does he ignore you or is he actively cruel?

I can shed some light on this by telling you there is a reason people put other people down in public. They do it because they have low self-esteem. How simple: Put someone down, build yourself up. One very common way of playing this out is for boyfriends or girlfriends to do it to their partners in front of their friends. It's like they are saying, "Look at me, I have the upper hand in the relationship." Another reason for doing this, though, is that they feel they don't have the upper hand, because they feel like they have lost control, and they care too much. One way for them to balance this out is to make statements or behave in such a way that makes them feel like they aren't weak and controlled by the other person. Is this making sense to you?

They feel powerless. They are so in love/attached/ in need of you that they are embarrassed by it. They don't want their friends to see how vulnerable they are around you, so they act all tough.

What you need to figure out is this: How bad is the problem?

For example: Now that you know what motivates him to behave this way, you see that it is really harmless. It's really no big deal.

Or: This is bad. He does it all the time, and it is painful and humiliating for you. You have tried to talk to him about it, and he just yells and gets defensive.

If you conclude that he doesn't respect you, be strong and end the relationship. Remember, we all deserve to be treated with respect. Oftentimes, the person we are with does not know about respect. You actually help everyone involved when you insist on being treated right. You help yourself by doing the thing that builds character, and you help the other person by teaching him that we all deserve to be treated well.

# My Boyfriend Loves Me More Than I Love Him

♥

The giving of love is an education in itself.

Eleanor Roosevelt

*Dear Kim,*

*What do you do when you are in a relationship with someone who loves you more than you love him? I like my boyfriend, and I even love him. He is always talking about our future, though, in a way I can't relate to. I don't think I will be with him forever. I feel bad when he talks like this, and I can't say anything back to him. Should I break up with him?*

I don't think you need to end the relationship. Look, the fact that two people even end up together is a miracle. I think it is expecting too much to think that you both will feel exactly the same way.

I have a friend who has been in a relationship for a very long time. When they first got together, she felt he loved her more, and, at times, she felt he loved her too much. It made her feel suffocated and controlled. Then, after a time, things happened that made her feel scared and vulnerable, and he was there for her. She then realized how grateful she was that he loved her as much as he did. A while later, they both went to look at colleges. When they got back home, he seemed more excited to go than she was. Now she felt like she loved him more. She was very sad about leaving him. Today, they are still together, and the scales go back and forth.

To me, this is the definition of a relationship. Sometimes, one person is more secure and confident, and then it changes. Being able to roll with this and not get stuck on one side or the other is the key to a long and happy union.

# How Do I Save Our Relationship?

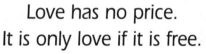

Love has no price.
It is only love if it is free.

Melody Beattie

Dear Kim,

I have been with the same girl for about three years. We have broken up about five times, but we keep getting back together. We love each other, but I wonder if we are good for each other because we fight and we hurt each other a lot.

I am thinking we should move on, but when I mention it to her she just cries. What should we do? I really don't know what I want anymore.

Are you guys *in love,* or are you just very attached to one another? There is a difference. Attached is not wanting to be without the other person. Love is wanting to be with the other person. It can be subtle, but the difference is big.

When two people have been together as long as you two have, it becomes horribly painful to think of your life without the other. It also becomes easy to blame the other for what is wrong with your life. These two things sound like opposites, but they are two sides of the same coin: attachment.

Love is about wanting to be together but being okay when you are apart. It is about looking inside when there is a problem and asking what you can do to make this better, or asking what you are not understanding about your girlfriend or boyfriend.

With love also comes the ability to let go when it is time to do so.

Do you guys have a way to work through problems?

Do you discuss disagreements?

When one is hurt, does the other try to understand why? And listen rather than defend?

Do you get caught up in who is right and who is wrong, rather than what is best for *us?*

Are you able to speak your truth to one another, even if it is hurtful?

Do you make sure the other person knows he or she has been heard and understood when you are discussing things?

These are questions about things we all do, and don't do.

They are also guidelines for how to improve a relationship that is stuck. If you are stuck in a yucky place with your girlfriend or boyfriend and you really want to work it out the first thing you have to know is that it will take:

- Time
- Patience
- Feeling some pain

If you are both willing, agree to spend time *talking* and *listening*.

One person begins.

That person talks about *how he or she is feeling!*

For example, "I get hurt when you just walk by me at school when you are with your buddies."

The other should say: "I understand that it hurts when I ignore you when I'm with my buddies."

Then it's his turn: "When I am with my buddies I am embarrassed for them to see me all sweet with you."

She says: "I understand that when you are with your friends you feel embarrassed to be all sweet with me."

*It is important that there is real understanding here. So each person takes a minute to think about where the other person is coming from. Oftentimes, we jump ahead to our own defense or our own needs rather than just taking one minute to fully understand what the other is feeling and experiencing and* trying *to communicate.*

The whole thing will go south if one of you gets defensive. The following is an example of what I mean when I say defensive:

"I can't stop and talk to you when I am on my way to

practice. You are being ridiculous. You are too demanding of me."

This kind of talk will make it worse, yet this is what we all do when we feel like we are being made wrong.

Once you have gone over all the things that upset and/or bother each of you, you will find that you are both feeling lighter, happier and much more in love.

It is so important in relationships to feel that you have been heard and understood. We often think the problem is about someone being right and someone being wrong, and it becomes a competition to determine who is right. The truth is, when you are only talking about your feelings you are always right because they are *your* feelings. (Of course, this is true of other people if they are only talking about *their* feelings.)

Pointers to remember:

*Listening* is the most important relationship skill.

*Understanding* the other person's feelings will always result in improving the relationship.

*It isn't a competition;* it is a partnership.

As long as you talk about yourself and your feelings and don't attack or blame, you don't need to worry about being wrong.

When we don't have this kind of communication in relationships, all this stuff piles up. The heart becomes weighted down with hurt and anger, and it can't feel the love that is there. Remember, this stuff doesn't happen overnight. But every time you remember to use this type of communication, the payoff is huge.

# We Are So Different

*Dear Kim,*

*I have a question for you. I have been going out with Ryan for five months, and I love him very much. It is just that I have more fun hanging out with my friends.*

*I get all excited when we are going to see each other and look forward to it for days, but when I am actually with him I don't always have fun. All he ever wants to do is make out, and when we aren't doing that, he just wants to watch TV or go to a movie. I feel like talking and laughing and going for walks, but none of this is interesting to him. I am afraid we are headed for a breakup, and I don't want that . . . at least I don't think I do. What should I do?*

What you are feeling is a common thing. It is partly due to the differences between guys and girls. I have put together a list of some of those differences. This list is the result of asking hundreds of teenagers for their opinions.

Girls are very romantic. They like to talk about love.

Guys are very shy when it comes to talking about their feelings.

Girls like to discuss problems. They like to talk about their problems with just about anyone who will listen. They especially like to discuss these things with their boyfriend.

Guys do not like to discuss their problems. They especially don't like to discuss them with their girlfriend. They feel that it isn't cool to even *have* problems, let alone discuss them.

Guys love to feel needed.

Girls love to feel beautiful and adored.

Girls feel safe when their boyfriend is strong and confident.

Guys feel good when their girlfriend feels safe with them.

Girls like to give advice and think it makes them helpful and therefore more lovable.

Guys don't like to get advice from their girlfriend because they feel like it means she thinks he can't solve things on his own.

Girls feel better after talking to their friends about their problems.

Guys feel better after solving their problems on their own.

Girls, even though they say they want love and attention, have a difficult time receiving these things.

Guys have an equally difficult time giving. They aren't selfish; they are frightened of doing something wrong.

Guys feel bad when girls are unhappy. They fear it is their fault.

Girls tend to exaggerate their problems by saying things like *never* and *always*. They are just trying too hard to be understood.

This might be one of the most important ones in this list:

When things are going great in a relationship, guys like to back away for a while. Girls, of course, think this means they don't love them anymore, and they get upset. The more upset they get, the more the guy wants to back away.

Girls: Try to let the guy back away without freaking out, and he will come back to you more in love with you than he was before. When a guy needs his space, a girl should just hang with her girlfriends, or do something she enjoys, and let him be. The guy will be so impressed that she didn't get all weird that he will think she is the best thing that ever happened to him.

Guys: If a guy can listen when his girlfriend is upset and not get defensive, holding her and telling her everything will be okay, then she will think he is the best thing that ever happened to her.

Remember, we are very different and we are also the same. We all have feelings, and we all want to feel loved. That is the bottom line. This list isn't for playing games or manipulating your partner. It is so you can better understand the person you love and do a better job of making that person feel special and happy.

# I'm Tired of Being Compared to Other Guys

♥

Always be a first-rate version
of yourself, instead of a second-rate
version of somebody else.

Judy Garland

*Dear Kim,*

*My girlfriend always compares me to her friends'
boyfriends. Needless to say, this drives me crazy. I am me,
and I kinda would like that to be enough.*

I understand how you feel. Comparing is often an
invitation to unhappiness.

I recently read somewhere that people seldom have

their expectations met in relationships. I will take it a step further and say . . . *never*. Our expectations can't be met because they are always unrealistic.

I have been guilty of having high expectations myself. I remember one day I was with my girlfriend, and I was going on about how my boyfriend (at the time) wasn't doing this and that, and I was all upset about it. I was sure that other guys were more thoughtful or more generous, and I was the one who got stuck with the loser. She joined in and starting complaining about her boyfriend, saying *he* was in fact the worst. He never brought her flowers or took her out to romantic dinners. And then, for no apparent reason, she just started laughing out loud. I joined in, and we could not stop. We were laughing hysterically. We both realized how silly we were being. I think she said it first: "Hey, it isn't like we're perfect or anything." In that moment we realized we were being unrealistic in our expectations. We wanted our boyfriends to be *perfect*.

So, to answer your question:

Comparing boyfriends or girlfriends is dangerous territory. Usually, we are comparing them to something that doesn't even exist.

John never yells at Sally.

Dan always calls Sue when he says he will.

Adam is so romantic.

*Dangerous territory.*

If I were you, I would tell your girlfriend that if she wants to discuss something about the relationship that is upsetting to her, then you would be happy to listen.

But when she starts throwing comparisons at you in order to change you, nothing could be more ineffective.

Tell her it just makes you feel bad and even angry. These are not emotions that promote romantic behavior. Once again, be sure to let her know you are open to hearing what her dissatisfactions are, just in a more constructive way.

The bottom line is that we are who we are, and we all want to be accepted for just that, not someone else's idea of who we *could* be.

# We Just Had a Fight, and My Boyfriend Snapped

♥

The turning point in the
process of growing up is when you
discover the core strength within
you that survives all hurt.

Max Lerner

*Dear Kim,*

*I can hardly write this because my hands are shaking. My boyfriend and I just had a huge fight. I have never heard anyone scream like he did, and it really scared me . . . and hurt me. We were talking on the phone, and I was upset with him. I knew I was kind of being harsh, but I was really hurt by something he did and I was mad. I wasn't screaming, though. All of a sudden, he just started screaming so loud and then he hung up. Right before he hung up, he broke up with me, but I don't know for sure if he meant it.*

*What should I do?*

Fighting is so hard. You feel so bad afterward, and nobody is the winner. It sounds to me like you have a good idea as to why it happened and that you are just shocked that he got as angry as he did. I guess I would be, too.

I would wait for him to apologize. Even though you may have been egging him on a bit, he owes you an apology for letting it go to that extreme.

Once he has apologized, I think it would be a good idea to have a talk about it. You can say you are sorry for your part and then try to figure out a better way for each of you to communicate.

For instance, you can say, "The next time I am upset about something like this, what would be the best way for me to let you know?" And then go from there.

We all have buttons that get pushed, and we don't always know what other people's are until we run into a situation like yours. I think you may need a little time to heal from the fight, so be sure to do something nice for yourself.

If fighting becomes a regular thing, I would think about whether or not you want to stay with him. Bad tempers can be a scary thing and can leave someone so uptight and frightened that the relationship no longer is capable of being an equal one. One time certainly does not mean that this is the way it is going to be. You will know when it has become a problem. It goes without saying that if his temper *ever* drives him to hit you or become physically abusive in *any* way (a shove, a push, *anything!*), it is good-bye time.

# I'm Finally Happy. . . . Can It Last?

*Dear Kim,*

*I spent the last two years of my life hopelessly and tragically in love with a guy who played me like a yo-yo. Come here, go away, come here, go away. I was always available, and I was always getting dumped soon thereafter. Let's face it, he had no respect for me.*

*I was finally able to let go and move on. I am now in a new relationship and it appears to be very sane and smooth.*

*Do you have any advice for how to keep it that way?*

First, I want to congratulate you for being able to move on. It isn't easy to leave someone when you have been together for a long time. You can feel good that you are now choosing healthier relationships. It is a sign that you are getting healthier, too.

What you said about him not respecting you was a very keen observation on your part. I am sure you know that, to a certain degree, you didn't respect yourself, either. It is important for you to see the part you played in the lack of respect between the two of you. You can't change him, but you *can* change yourself, and it sounds like you are well on your way.

As for keeping the relationship you are in now in good shape, the key is to take care of yourself and to *respect yourself.* Although this is going to sound weird, the best way to begin to change this behavior is to continually ask yourself what would be the most self-respectful thing to do in this situation? As strange as this sounds, I still do it today. Remember we are all striving for the same thing here.

Here's an example of what I am talking about:

You and your boyfriend have a fight. You guys have plans to go out that night, but when he hangs up the phone he says to you, "And you can forget about seeing me tonight, our date is off!"

An hour later, and five minutes before you were going to go out, he calls and says he will be there in an hour to pick you up. What should you do?

Before I answer this, let me be honest and say that, when I was your age, if I really liked this guy I would have said, "Okay, I'll be waiting." However, as I am sure you have already figured out, this is not what someone with a lot of self-respect would do.

Don't be mad or mean, but say to him, "I am sorry, but I made other plans when you called the date off. Maybe we can get together tomorrow." Trust me, I know this isn't always the easiest thing to do, but he will not be so quick to make threats next time, and he might even hang in there until you guys have worked out whatever it is you are fighting about.

Bottom line, remember we are striving for self-respect. Nobody is perfect, but we are trying to treat ourselves in the best way possible.

# Shadows Dance

BECCA WOOLF

*The past merges with the present to create the future.*
*The reflection of a genuine true love on the darkness*
*of past loss creates a glowing light where*
*shadows can dance.*

Two shadows dance along beneath
the yellow moon tonight.
Two hearts that beat as one
like the flickering of light.
I used to dance without him,
a soul lost from before.
Afraid to love another
with a heart so strifed and sore.
But tears run dry I realized
and new tides to sweep away
the past that left you hopeless,
and the dawn of a new day.
My dance is to a different song
A shadow as my guide.

The darkness of a brand-new light
that I don't have to hide
Young love is ephemeral
burning bright and soon to die
But losing love has made me stronger
and new hearts have captured I.
Two shadows dance along beneath
the yellow moon tonight
The light that burns so brightly
in the darkness of the night.

"He's my new boyfriend.
I know he's cold and unemotional, but, on the other hand,
he never criticizes me, he doesn't complain about my
friends, and if things don't work out,
he'll be gone in the spring!"

*Reprinted by permission of Randy Glasbergen.*

# I Don't Trust My Boyfriend

♥

Until we learn
whichever life lesson we're
meant to at the time—self-acceptance,
self-determination, self-discipline,
self-esteem, self-forgiveness,
self-interest, self-knowledge,
self-respect, self-sufficiency
or self-worth—our lessons will
keep coming back to us.

Sarah Ban Breathnach

*Dear Kim,*

*I've got a problem, and I don't know if it is my fault or my boyfriend's fault.*

*I don't feel like I can trust him, and it is getting worse, not better.*

*About six months ago, I found out he was not being honest with me. He was dating his ex when I thought he was out with the guys. When he told me about it, he said that it had only happened once. He told me that he was missing her, and they went out. But he said nothing happened and that was that. Then as we talked more he told me that, actually, he had seen her three times. (She lives in another town.) He promised me he would never do this again and said he loved me and only me. I believe him, but I can't trust him. What should I do?*

This is a very hard question to answer. There is a part of me that wants to say: dump him. He is a liar, and a liar is a liar. But, things aren't always black and white. People do make mistakes that they are sorry for. There are people who do something like this and never do it again. There are also people who you just can't trust. They justify their behavior and really don't think there is anything wrong with it.

You have to figure out which kind of person he is. I can tell you still care for him and that you want to hang in there. But you make a good point. Is it your fault you have trouble trusting him or is it his? In order for me to answer this I have a question: When you get scared that he is lying, how does he respond?

I think this is very telling. Hopefully he is sweet and kind to you at these moments. Hopefully he says that he understands he damaged the trust you had for him and he will be patient as you heal. If he doesn't have this attitude, then I think he is not deserving of your love.

The thing about love and relationships is that there usually aren't yes-and-no answers to the questions that arise. Things aren't always black and white, good or bad, right or wrong. With this in mind, I think the most important things to remember are:

- Respect yourself.
- Listen to your heart; it tells no lies.
- Listen to your friends but know that *you* are the one who has to live with your decisions.
- Avoid thinking in terms of "making mistakes" or "right and wrong."

Do what you have to do. You will indeed make mistakes, but guess what? Everyone does. I have made thousands. The important thing is that we learn from our mistakes and we begin to develop an inner trust. We have to look at things with softer eyes and see them as learning experiences. This is what we mean when we talk about self-love and acceptance.

# I'm Always Worried He'll Find Someone Better

*Dear Kim,*

    *I have been in a relationship with Derek for four months, and I love him very much. He is very popular and all the girls like him. I know this should make me proud and all that, but, instead, I just worry all the time that he is going to leave me for someone prettier or more popular.*

    *I know it doesn't do anything for the relationship for me to be jealous and insecure all the time, but I can't help it. Sometimes I wish he were ugly or something so I didn't have to be scared all the time of losing him.*

Yeah, I know what you mean. You want a great guy, but then when you have one you are always afraid someone is looking to steal him away. The sad thing is, you are probably right.

So, what to do:

First of all, try not to lay this on him too much. Guys don't like to have to reassure you on a daily basis that they love you and only you.

When you get scared, talk about it with your girlfriends. Hopefully by talking about it with them you can relax and recover.

Try to remember that you are good enough for your boyfriend, and there is no reason he would want anyone else. This is strange, but *the more you can come from this place, the more secure he will feel that he has made the right choice.* It is one of those catch-22 situations: If you are too insecure and too worried and he is aware of this, it could become a self-fulfilling prophecy. The best thing you can do is believe in your heart that you are all he could ever ask for.

# *Fear*

MEREDEE SWITZER

---

If our love is only a will to
possess, it is not love.

Thich Nhat Hanh

---

The new girl at school was from Alaska. I didn't even know her, and I already despised her. It was the usual routine at school that day. The assembling of my circle of friends at break was the same, except the banter was different. They were buzzing about this *girl* from Alaska, and half of them didn't even know her name. From what they were saying, though, she was gorgeous. My boyfriend, Justin, finally informed us that her name was July. Justin, of all people, was talking about her the most and how she was in four of his classes now. They had all come to conclude that she was awesome. Immediately, I became insanely envious of this *girl* I'd never met.

From then on, my jealousy only worsened. Justin, *my* boyfriend, had invited her to a football game and a tour of the town. I resented that he didn't even recognize how this affected me. He didn't even invite *me* along. After all, it was perfectly innocent to him. But in the eyes of a concerned girlfriend it was anything but innocent. *Who asked him to be the welcome-wagon anyway?*

One night, she was over at his house when I called. They were alone. I told Justin how I felt, and he didn't get it. So, I decided to make an unforeseen visit and finally see this evil man-stealing enchantress for myself. Except when I got there, she didn't look like a man-stealer. In fact, she looked like someone who could be my friend, which made my stomach turn circles even more. The guys were right, she was beautiful, and the confirmation killed me. I discussed my agitation with my boyfriend, but he still didn't understand why his friendship with her bothered me so much. I gave up.

The words that exited Justin's mouth next were the sweetest sound to my ears. He proceeded to tell me that July was interested in his best friend, Matt. She wanted to ask him out. What relief this gave me! What was even better was that, of course, Matt liked her, too, and they became an item. Now that all my feelings of betrayal and hatred for her were lost, I opened up and asked her to go shopping with me the next day. She hadn't made many girlfriends since she moved here. Before long, we had become the best of friends. Parties, shopping, Homecoming and friends—we had a lot in common. I had some of the best and worst times of my life with her. Since then, we have moved on from those boyfriends. They remained friends, we remained friends. Soon, July and I drifted apart. She changed schools, and I stayed busy. Some things are better now, others are worse. I have learned that friendships will bring me many lessons in life. I can only hope to grasp these lessons before they pass me by. It was silly to be afraid of July. Sometimes the things you fear most are not worth fearing at all and are often the things you grow to love.

# The Love of My Life Moved Away

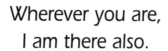

Wherever you are,
I am there also.

Ludwig van Beethoven

*Dear Kim,*

*I loved her like I have never loved anyone before. She was everything to me. I didn't care what happened as long as I could be with her. She made everything okay.*

*One day she told me her family was moving, and I thought I would never be okay again. My parents told me it was not healthy to love someone so much, yet I knew it wasn't healthy to have to live without her. She felt like my life force, and I was truly scared what would happen to me without her to hold me.*

*She called me last night and it was the first time I have talked to her without hanging up and crying. My friends say that I am starting to return to my old self again.*

*I really don't want to love like that again, but I am feeling like I am ready to at least go out on a date. Everyone knows what I have been through, and they are very supportive of me. I just don't know what to do next.*

My heart felt sad reading your letter. I am sorry that you had to hurt so much.

I would take it real slow if I were you. Maybe go out with a group of friends. Or ask a girl out, but just don't push yourself. You will heal, and you will love again.

When I was young we moved every two years. I had to leave a boyfriend that I was very much in love with once. It was very hard, and I chose to deal with it in some "less than intelligent" ways. I tried to punish my parents for making us move, but in turn just ended up hurting myself. (I started hanging out with "the bad kids.") It didn't take long for me to get back on track, but I tell you this so you will remember that no one "did this to you." It actually sounds like you are doing well. Hang in there.

Know that you are okay just as you are. If you do start dating, just remember to take things slow and not give too much of yourself away.

# My Parents Don't Approve of My Boyfriend

♥
_____

Tiny choices mean tiny changes.
But it is only with infinitesimal
change, changes so small no one else
even realizes you're making them,
that you have any hope for
transformation.

Leo Tolstoy

_____

Dear Kim,

I am in tenth grade and am in the first relationship of my life. I have had a very hard time up until now because every guy that I liked didn't like me and vice versa. Now I finally have a boyfriend, and my parents don't approve *of him. They think he is not good enough for me, but they don't even know him. He is a great guy. They are upset because of how he looks. They don't realize how unfair this is. You have to help me; this is so unfair.*

I have to agree with you if, in fact, your parents are only judging him on appearances. I suggest you try to discuss this with them in a very specific way.

Tell them you would like to talk to them. Ask if you can set a time when they will be able to sit and talk for at least thirty minutes. Ask that it be a time with no distractions. Explain to them that it is very important to you. Hopefully they will agree.

When it comes time to talk, try to be very calm. Know what you are going to say to them.

Explain to them that it is very hard for you to be going through this with them. Be sure to not attack them in any way, i.e., don't say, "This is stupid and unfair." Just tell them how you feel.

For example:

"I really want you to give him a chance. I only ask that you get to know him before judging him. He makes me very happy and treats me very respectfully."

Make a deal with them that you will listen to what they have to say if they will agree to meet him and talk to him first.

In other words, see if you can negotiate with them.

Let them know that you understand their concerns and you appreciate them. Give them examples, for instance, "He is the first guy who isn't just putting the moves on me" (if this is true). Tell them his *good* qualities. Hopefully they will agree to discussing this and then meeting him.

For your part, listen openly to what they have to say about him.

There are times when parents make mistakes and it is possible that they are unfairly judging him—but there are also times when they are right. In order for this to work, *both* sides need to listen and be open-minded.

"Your date will be here soon.
It's time to spin the Wheel of Curfew!"

# My Boyfriend Ignored Me at a Party

♥

When a woman is speaking
to you, listen to what she
says with her eyes.

Victor Hugo

*Dear Kim,*

*The other night, my boyfriend and I went to a party together. I was very excited because this was one of the first times we would be out together other than by ourselves on a date. I couldn't wait to dance with him and meet some of his friends.*

*When we got to the party, he just walked away from me and went up to his guy friends. Whenever I tried to hang with him, he would just walk away, almost like he didn't even know me.*

*When it was time to leave I was pretty upset and didn't*

*even know what to say. When we were driving home he reached over to hold my hand, and I just jerked away from him. Then he acted all sweet and couldn't understand what my problem was.*

*When I finally had the nerve to tell him what was wrong, he acted shocked.*

*He said, "We're together all the time. I just thought that since I was going to be with you later I would hang with my friends and you would be with yours. Sorry." He was kind of sarcastic, and he made me feel like a jerk for being upset. Now I don't know what to think.*

I can see why you are confused.

Whenever you have a problem like this, there is a good technique for getting clear. When trying to evaluate what happened, do the following either with a friend or on a piece of paper:

- First look at what actually happened. Be like a camera. No feelings, no opinions: just what happened.

  For instance: I arrived at the party. Jake and I walked in together. Jake then walked over to his friends. I stood there for two minutes. Then I went to my friends, etc. Just keep going like this until the end.

- Now that you have done the first step, go back and find the first moment you felt something. Continue on to each time you had feelings about something.

For instance: I was happy when we walked in the door. I was sad when he walked away. I was embarrassed when he walked away a second time. I was mad when he didn't answer my question.

Once again, try to keep it honest. For instance, if you say, "I was mad when he judged me," this is not objective because you don't know what he was feeling. Instead say, "I was mad when he said, 'Don't be ridiculous.' It felt to me like he was judging me." The honesty is for *you*. Our minds have a bad habit of making things worse than they actually are. We all do it.

Now that you have done these two things, you are clear about what happened and how you felt. This is the best way to figure things out.

Remember: No one else should tell you that your feelings are stupid, ridiculous or wrong.

This is how you feel. Ask that he understand that. Many times, our feelings are exaggerated or even paranoid, but the best way to work through this is to be honest about how you felt and then listen to his side of the story.

I wasn't there, so I don't know what happened. The point is that your feelings got hurt and you felt ignored. Hopefully, he can hear this without being defensive.

You should try to hear his side also. He may say, "I feel funny hanging all over my girlfriend at a party." Guys are different than girls in this way. They often have a hard time being affectionate in public. They can feel vulnerable and weak when they show their feelings for a girl in front of others.

The challenge is to understand each other's feelings and hopefully come to some resolve. He can say, "Next time I won't ignore you completely, but don't expect me to be with you the whole time."

You can agree or not. You might say, "I don't want to go to a party with you under those circumstances."

Remember to compromise and to be honest.

Most important, don't ever feel bad for the way you feel.

# My Boyfriend Pays More Attention to My Parents Than to Me!

♥

The greatest happiness in life
is the conviction that we are loved—
loved for ourselves, or rather,
loved in spite of ourselves.

Victor Hugo

*Dear Kim,*

*My boyfriend and I have been together for a year now, which is a very long time at my age. When we first started going out my parents didn't like him very much, but after a while they began to accept him. When he comes over to my house now, my dad and Richard will sit and watch basketball together or talk about some other boring thing, and I can't help but think it was better when they didn't like him. I know this doesn't make sense, but he kind of tries too hard to get their approval and I seem to be the least important thing to him. My mom thinks I am being silly, but she thinks anything I say or think is silly so she is no help. The thing is, sometimes I dread it when he is going to come over. It just isn't that much fun anymore. What should I do?*

There are really two issues here and I want to address them both.

The first is how you feel about your boyfriend.

The second is your relationship with your mom.

I will start with your boyfriend. It sounds to me like you might not have as much respect for him as you did in the–beginning. Perhaps you are growing apart. My guess is that things are cooling off and he isn't "the one" to you anymore.

Think about it. Oftentimes, we like someone better when there is external resistance, like the kind you were getting from your parents. That is another thing to consider. I have no way of knowing if this is true in this case. No matter what the case, you should talk to him and tell him it kind of bugs you that he acts the way he does around your dad. Could you be jealous because he isn't giving you all the attention? This is another possibility.

Whatever it is, you know the answer. My advice is to

listen to what it is and then decide what you want to do about it.

As for issue number two, I would imagine it is very hurtful to you that your mom says your feelings are silly. My mom used to say that to me, and I hated it. It felt like she didn't understand what I was feeling and it felt like she was saying my feelings weren't important. Her intentions were to help me. She thought by saying that it was silly, I would not take it seriously, and, therefore, not feel pain. Mothers would prefer us to feel no pain, you know. (Now that I am a mother I understand this.)

You could tell her, without yelling or anything, that your feelings aren't silly, they are very real for you. If you say it the right way, she will hear you. It is common for girls your age to want to talk to your friends more than to your mom. But, being a mother, I can tell you we love to be confided in. Just tell her that in order for you to want to do that she has to listen and not judge what you are feeling. I hope all this works out for you; it sounds like you are ready for some changes in your life.

# Can Our Cyber-Love Be for Real?

♥

The best and most beautiful
things in the world cannot be seen,
nor touched . . . but are
felt in the heart.

Helen Keller

*Dear Kim,*

*I am in love with a guy I met online. Before you judge me and say that it isn't possible to love someone you have never met, let me tell you more.*

*I am a freshman in high school, and I am not the most popular girl in the world. In fact, I'm not popular at all. I'm not beautiful, and I'm not skinny like girls in magazines. Because of this, I don't have guys chasing after me or even talking to me for that matter.*

*When I come home from school, I do my homework and*

*then go online. It is a place where I have lots of friends and people don't judge me by the way I look. They like me because I am smart and funny and nice. A couple of months ago I started talking to this guy and we hit it off right away. After a couple of weeks, we decided we liked each other, and now we even say "I love you" to each other when we chat.*

*My parents were worried he could be some creep, but he sent me his picture and I have talked to him on the phone a couple of times. He is so nice to me, and we have a lot in common. He is also lonely and has never had a "real" girlfriend.*

*My parents have backed off now, and they even let us talk on the phone on the weekends. He lives far away but he has been talking lately about coming to visit over the summer.*

*This is very exciting to me but also scary. I don't want to lose what we have, and I am afraid he might not like me if he meets me. I am also afraid I might not like him. I don't know if he is actually going to come visit, but I am not sure what I should say when he talks about it.*

I have heard many stories of cyber-romance. There are as many different possibilities for things to go right or wrong as there are in "real" romance.

As is true anytime you like someone, many things could happen. There are never any guarantees.

An online relationship has limits. You don't know what the other person looks like, how that person acts in person or if you will hit it off when you finally do meet. You can exchange pictures, talk on the phone and even make a video tape for each other. These are ways you can get to know each other a little better before meeting.

The most dangerous thing about this arrangement is the possibility of someone lying about who they are. Since you have spoken to him on the phone and you have seen a picture of him it is unlikely that he is lying. (I guess someone could fake these things, but we will assume he isn't doing that.)

Do you ever call him? It is important to make sure that he isn't the only one calling.

Also, you might want to talk to his parents as another safety measure.

So, assuming he is who he says he is, just take things one step at a time.

If he is going to come visit and it is an agreeable arrangement for you and your parents, then just see what happens. (I would suggest that if he does come visit he have another place to stay.) If it doesn't work out, it won't be the first time a relationship hasn't. No matter what the circumstances are there will always be risks.

If you decide you don't want him to visit then tell him. Just take it one step at a time, be honest with yourself and then be honest with him.

I am not against cyber-love as a way to experience relationships and explore those feelings. I would suggest that you be open to a relationship with someone you know and live near, though, as well. Try not to close off other possibilities, because, no matter how you look at it, a long-distance relationship is a very difficult thing to maintain.

"Romeo and Juliet met online in a chat room.
But their relationship ended tragically
when Juliet's hard drive died."

*Reprinted by permission of Randy Glasbergen.*

# My Virtual Relationship Is Real to Me

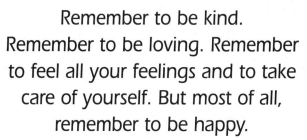

Remember to be kind.
Remember to be loving. Remember
to feel all your feelings and to take
care of yourself. But most of all,
remember to be happy.

Melody Beattie

Dear Kim,

I am currently involved with a girl I met on the Internet. My friends make fun of me because they say it is a fake relationship. Although we have met and gone out, it was only twice and the rest of our relationship has been online. They think it is stupid because we are not *physically together and therefore not able to do physical things. They can't figure out why I would bother.*

*I am hoping you can shine some light on this and tell them how shallow they are being.*

First of all, there are lots of Internet relationships. I think it is limited in some ways, but very cool in others. When a relationship takes place like this, communication is a huge part of what is happening. I think this is good.

I have previously mentioned the safety measures that are necessary so I won't do that again. I would imagine the two of you have talked about many things and have come to know each other well.

Don't let your friends bug you, and besides what do they know about the possibilities? Word to the wise: Don't knock it till you've tried it.

*Nine*

# Breaking Up Is Hard to Do

*The human spirit is stronger
than anything that can
happen to it.*

C. C. Scott

# *Breaking Up Is Hard to Do*

♥
_____

Losing in love is like losing
in chess; the more you play, the
more you learn.

Lia Gay
_____

I think few things are as painful as the end of a relationship. When a relationship ends it is a mini-death. It
marks the end of shared love, the end of something that
has become a part of you. This end is filled with grief,
anger, rejection and depression. Even in cases where
one or both parties feel a sense of relief because something that caused pain is now over, they still must go
through a period of grieving.

Breakups come in many ways. You can be left, or you
can be the one who leaves. You can find out directly or
indirectly, like finding your love with someone else.

People break up by writing letters, by phone or in person. It can be a slow death or a fast one. No matter how it happens, it hurts.

In this chapter, we will hear about some of these endings and how they were handled. If you are currently nursing your wounds from the loss of a relationship, finding out that you aren't alone will ease the pain a little. The most important thing you will get from this chapter and from life experience is the knowledge that this, too, will pass.

# For Zack

BRANDY NICHOLAS

Ink spreading across
the page, we spoke
once again of embracing
each other in a moment
of vanilla and nightfall.

The days are all alike:
sorrow filling our hearts,
tears forming in my eyes,
a cloud falling upon us.
We were learning to
love, open up, to take
matters into our own
hands.

The hope held us tight.
For six months my heart
soared. Its wings
stretching and spreading.

But these moments are
finished, as we opened the
door, tangled with
emotions, we whispered
Good-bye.

# *My First Heartbreak*

ANONYMOUS

The affirmation of one's own life,
happiness, growth, freedom,
is rooted in one's capacity to love.

Erich Fromm

I had been in a relationship with Jason for a while. We got along pretty well and we hardly ever fought. He called me every night at 8:00 P.M., and he always had time for me on the weekends. Many of my girlfriends said they only wanted a boyfriend like Jason, then they would be happy. When I heard this I would remind myself how lucky I really was. The problem was I just didn't feel that way anymore.

It was a Thursday night, and I had just returned home from drama rehearsal. I was tired and had a ton of homework and became short with my parents when they questioned me about my day. I was sitting on my bed feeling guilty about the way I had snapped at them when the phone rang.

I remember being surprised to hear Jason on the other end of the phone line because it was just 7:30 and he was usually so predictable.

I snapped at him, too. "I can't talk, Jason, I want to get some homework done first. Why don't you call me back at 8:00 like you do every night?"

"Cindy, we need to talk." Now I knew what my parents meant when they said they didn't like my tone of voice. I certainly didn't like his.

"What's going on, Jason?" I asked.

"Cindy, we need to break up. We aren't happy anymore; we're just going through the motions. I don't want to stay together until we start hating each other, and I think that is where we are headed."

I started crying so hard that I couldn't talk to him. Finally, when I was just unable to stop crying, I told him I had to go. He didn't even argue, he just said, "Okay," and hung up.

I knew he was right but that didn't make it hurt any less; in fact, I think it made it worse.

The next day at school I kept thinking he would run up and say it was all a big mistake but he didn't, and as the day went on I felt worse than I had ever felt. There was no drama, no fighting, just a deafening silence that echoed in my head saying, "It's over, Cindy, it's over."

All my efforts seemed to go unnoticed: the new clothes,

laughing extra loud when he was around and flirting ruthlessly with all his friends. One day he even said he was happy to see that I was okay, and he hoped that I would be able to find happiness with someone else. He really didn't care anymore.

On February 10 (I wrote it in my journal), I began to feel the pain lifting off my heart. On February 21, I got a phone call from someone I had recently noticed in my history class. We went out and had fun. It was the first time I had had fun in a very long time. A month later, I was able to have a conversation with Jason. I told him what I had known for a while, that breaking up was the right thing for us to do. I told him thanks for having the courage to do something I couldn't.

I told him that I hoped he was okay and that someday he would find someone else that he could be happy with. He was my first love and I will never forget him, but it felt great to be able to say those things and mean them.

# Untrue Love

SARA CORBIN

Were you there the day the music died?
Did you want to hold me when I cried?
Did you fight to stand there by my side
When I was in despair?

Did you keep me safe within your arms?
Did you protect me from all harm?
Or did you win me over with your charm,
Running fingers through my hair?

Did you simply see your chance
To get what you wanted with one dance?
You saw me hurting with one glance
And decided to fool my heart.

And like a fool I went along.
When we danced I sang the songs.
I never thought I could be wrong,
So I gladly played my part.

And now I lie here, wondering why
I ever thought that you and I
Could fall in love and never cry
Again for what we've done.

I'm terrified of the way I feel
Now that I know your love isn't real.
I'm not sure my heart will ever heal,
Because all I can do is run.

I run from the future, but mostly the past
Through the fields and the forest, so very fast.
Through the moonlight that midnight has cast
Onto my crying face.

I've prayed that you would decide to stay,
That I could keep you one more day,
And that you wouldn't turn away
And leave me in this place.

But I've fooled myself for much too long,
That our love was not a tragic song.
And I assume you will be gone,
No time left to borrow.

I'll try to smile when you say good-bye
And wait until you're gone to cry.
You'll be strong, and so will I
Although I feel such sorrow.

And so I'll face this world alone,
Cold as ice, and hard as stone,
Until a true love comes along.
I've nothing left to fear.

But when our love has long been dead,
When we've moved on to the road ahead,
And I'm lying wide awake in bed,
Your memory will be here.

# I Really Blew It, and Now I've Lost Him

♥

## The loving person has no need to be perfect, only human.

Leo Buscaglia

Dear Kim,

I used to have the sweetest, kindest, cutest, most incredible boyfriend in the whole world. I'm not kidding. He was so great, and I lost him. It was all my fault, which makes it so hard to live with.

He always thought about me and did such nice things for me. He brought me flowers, he called to say good night and he would plan really fun dates for us.

A couple of weeks ago we went to a party together and for some really stupid reason I started making out with a friend of his. Of course, I broke his heart and he left me.

I don't know why I did this, except for the fact that I

*didn't understand how good I had it. I guess you could say I took him for granted.*

*Now I can't do anything without being reminded of him. I turn on the radio and they are playing our song. I turn on the TV and there is a show we would watch together. He used to call me and we would watch* 90210 *or* Dawson's Creek *while staying on the phone. At school I always see him because we are in the same classes together. Everywhere I look I am reminded of him and how I blew it.*

*I have tried to apologize, but he acts like he is over me. He isn't mad or anything, he just says he doesn't need to be with someone who is as immature as I am. Trust me, that hurts. And he is right.*

*I wish there were something I could do or say. Please help me.*

You know how I am always saying love is the greatest teacher? Well, this is a great example. We all do stupid things and, yes, this was stupid. This is also how we learn. Unfortunately, if it didn't hurt as much as it does you might not learn never to do it again.

As for him, it may be too late. He just may not want to risk having this happen to him again, or he may just not have any feelings for you. If this is the case, you have to accept it. Painful, but true.

If there were a chance of you guys getting back

together, I would think it would only come with time. If I were you I would pull myself together and just try to be strong. Perhaps if he sees you taking care of yourself and being mature about it, he will see that you are changing and growing up. I think this is your only chance. It also is the best thing to do for you.

Don't beat yourself up. Like I said, we have all done things like this before. I made out with my boyfriend's brother once—*extremely stupid!* Okay, now do you feel better?

# Reunited:
# A Two-Sided Poem

BECCA WOOLF

I saw her today.
*I saw him today.*

It's been a while.
*It seems like centuries.*

She looked okay.
*I couldn't stop staring.*

We talked for a while.
*He looked so fine.*

She kept looking at me and I wondered why.
*He wouldn't look me in the eye and I wondered why.*

She asked me how I was and I told her about my
   new girlfriend.
*He asked me if I had a boyfriend, and I told him I didn't.*

I pretended like I cared.
*I pretended like I didn't care.*

She looked different than she used to.
*He looked better than ever.*

I gave her a friendly hug good-bye.
*We held each other one more time.*

And then I went surfing.
*And then I went home and cried.*

# She's Moved On, and I Can't Handle It

♥

The world is round and
the place which may seem like
the end may also be only
the beginning.

Joy Baker Priest

*Dear Kim,*

*When Ashley and I broke up, I was upset, but I thought I would be fine after a while. We both decided to end the relationship for lots of reasons. The thing is, when I see her at school, it kills me. I want to talk to her and hang out with her, and I can't. Today was awful because I saw her with another guy. I don't know how she got over us so quickly. I can't handle watching her be with someone else. What should I do?*

Breaking up with someone you love is never easy and never without pain.

The more you love someone, the more painful your feelings are. It will get easier, and there will even be a day when it won't bother you to see her with someone else. In the meantime, there are a few things you can do.

If there is a way you can walk to class where you won't see her, take that way for now. This will achieve two things: One is that you won't have to see her with another guy. The other is that she may be trying to make you jealous. If this is the case, it will drive her crazy that you aren't hanging around trying to see what she is up to.

Sorry, girls, but I have to tell him. . . .

Sometimes girls (guys do this, too) go out of their way to make guys jealous. Especially if the guy left her. You say that it was a mutual decision, but I am sure there is a part of her that wants you to miss her and want her back.

Whenever you break up with someone, there is always a period when it is very difficult and painful. I call it a grieving period, just like when someone dies. Because something has died: your relationship. The fact that you are so sad and having a difficult time tells me you are a caring person who was able to have a real loving relationship with someone. Remember, that is a good thing.

"You're really serious about not wanting to have
anything to do with me, aren't you?"

# *It Hurts So Much to Have Lost Him*

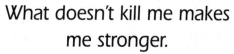

## What doesn't kill me makes me stronger.

### Wilhelm Friedrich Nietzsche

*Dear Kim,*

*I am so heartbroken right now I don't even know what to say. Michael and I have been together for almost a year, and he is everything to me. I love him so much, but he doesn't want to be with me anymore. He didn't even give me a reason. He just said it was better this way, and he just wanted for us to be friends. Kim, I feel like he ripped my heart out of my chest. I am in so much pain that it is hard to breathe. Please tell me what to do. I don't want to lose him.*

My heart breaks just hearing how much pain you are in. This is one of the hardest things you will ever have to go through.

I don't know if this is the first time someone has broken up with you, but my guess is that either it is, or this is the first time you have loved someone as much as you love Michael.

It is important to remember that this will pass. But it is also important that you let yourself feel the grief of losing someone you love.

Let yourself cry.

Listen to sad music.

Talk to your best friends.

I think it is okay to calmly ask Michael if he would talk to you about why he has decided to do this. It is important because, oftentimes, something like this happens because of a misunderstanding or untrue rumors. Assure him you will handle yourself and not make a scene if he will take the time to sit down with you and give you an honest explanation.

If it turns out that it isn't a misunderstanding and that he is just ready to move on, you have to accept that. Unfortunately, you cannot change how another person feels about you. This may well be the hardest of all life's lessons. I still struggle with it. The truth is, it is none of our business what another person is thinking or feeling about us. It is good to remember this, though, because we often think it is our business.

As heartbreaking as it is to have another person break up with you, it doesn't mean that you are unlovable. I know that you feel like that right now. Everyone does at these moments. But his choice does not make you any less lovable.

This is a time when you need your friends. Be sure to thank them for their time and support. Hang in there. This, too, shall pass. That is a promise.

# Love Lessons

### KELLY GARNETT

---

Since love is not a thing,
it is not lost when given. You can
offer your love completely to
hundreds of people and still retain
the same love you had originally.

Leo Buscaglia

---

I had always thought, when I went through the pain of breaking up with someone, that it was equally as hard for the person who was doing the breaking up as it was for the person receiving it. To know that I was going to hurt someone whom I cared for so deeply—to know that I would be the reason that person was going to be upset—was the most awful situation I had known . . . until I experienced the other side.

He was one of the most unique people I had ever known, which was why I liked him so much. There was just something about him that was special and unlike the rest of the guys at my school. He was passionate about everything that he did and if he loved something, he loved it with his whole heart.

And that was how he loved me. We dated for almost a year, but it was a year that was full of fights and confrontations. He and I wanted very different things out of our time together. I was his first serious relationship, and he was thrilled at the idea of spending every minute with me. It was my senior year, and I wanted to spend this time I had left doing things with all of my friends. He often accused me of not liking him as much as he liked me, and I would snap right back at him that he was trying to turn me into something I wasn't.

It was no surprise—in fact, somewhat of a relief— when we broke up at the end of that year. It was a mutual decision made by two people who were tired of hurting each other, and who realized they just couldn't make it work.

We spent the summer apart. He spent time with the guys, chasing after girls, being goofy and immature. I spent the summer doing a lot of thinking and planning as to where I wanted my future to go. We began to hang out again at the end of the three months.

He was very different. He seemed to have calmed down, to have relaxed. I enjoyed the time we spent together as we started over as friends—in fact I was surprised at just how much. I began to have feelings for him that I didn't have when we were dating. I wanted to be with him all the time.

When I realized that I was spending all of my time thinking about him and no one else, I knew I had to tell him. He had cared about me so much the first time we were together, I was sure that he would feel the same way and would want to give it another chance.

But I was wrong. He told me gently, but seriously, that he was tired of the "us." He loved being my friend and always would, but the idea of trying another relationship made him sad and unsure. He reminded me that our first attempt didn't go well, and was sure that trying again would only result in more heartbreak for both of us.

At that moment though, I would have taken any amount of heartbreak from a failed second chance in comparison to the way I felt. I felt empty and heartbroken and could not help crying tears that streamed down my face as I drove away. It was then that I realized who really got the worse end of the deal when feelings are one-sided. At least the one who makes the decision has a choice—I had no control over the way he felt. I could not do anything to change his mind. I simply had to accept the way things were and leave it at that.

All that was left for me was the big question: Was loving him worth the suffering I had to endure on both sides of heartbreak?

I felt better as the answer became clear to me. It was.

# It's So Hard

## BECCA WOOLF

It's so hard to say "I love you," and not draw back in
tears,

It's so hard to know that you're not there to help me face
my fears.

It's so hard to know the phone's at reach, but I cannot
hear your voice,

It's so hard to know that this time breaking up was not
my choice.

It's so hard to see you laughing when I'm crying deep
inside,

It's so hard to just find feelings and now have to make
them hide.

It's so hard to live without you, when I need you more
than words,

To want to scream how much I love you but hold back
and not be heard.

It's so hard to go to sleep at night when I cannot dream
of you,

It's so hard to think that you might fall in love with someone new.

It's so hard to not start crying when I hear your favorite song,

It's so hard to sit and wonder, where did I go wrong?

It's so hard to live without you, if I only would have known.

I will never love another, I would rather be alone.

# I Couldn't Wait for Her to Decide

♥
_____

You can't be brave if
you've only had wonderful things
happen to you.

Mary Tyler Moore

_____

*Dear Kim,*

*I just broke up with my girlfriend . . . like five minutes ago, so I am feeling pretty bad right now. She was all upset, but she is the one that started the whole thing. Last week we went to a party and there were lots of people there from another school. Kind of our rival school, but we party together. We were just hanging out and next thing I know she is totally flirting with this guy from the other school. She was laughing really loud at his stupid jokes and doing her whole thing that she does around guys. When we left I said something to her about it, and she didn't even deny it. She said, "I like him, he is really sweet." So I said, "Okay, do you want to be with him, because if you do just say the word." I thought she would tell me I was being silly but instead she said, "I want to think about it."*

*Well, I drove her home and needless to say that was the end of our "date."*

*All weekend I was so mad. I didn't call her and when she called me I didn't answer the phone.*

*Then I saw her at school on Monday. She was all sweet to me and asking me why I didn't call her back.*

*I just couldn't take it anymore, so tonight I broke up with her. I'm not going to sit around and wait for her to make up her mind. I just don't understand why she is the one freaking out now and crying and stuff. She acts like I am the one who did something mean.*

Can't have your cake and eat it, too. Sounds like she wants to have it all.

You did the right thing in my opinion.

I bet that this was pretty painful for you, but it is good that you are taking care of yourself by not letting her get away with it.

She sounds kind of immature, and it doesn't sound like you are interested in that kind of behavior. You should feel good that even though she doesn't know about respect yet, you do and you have it for yourself.

# Dried-Out Roses

BECCA WOOLF

Old red roses, dry and dead,
Wilted petals fall instead,
He once gave to me to keep.
Those days they lagged like lonely sleep,
And now they sit as time has passed,
Alone, without a love at last.
With shadows of our old love cry,
And wilted roses that won't die,
A phone with no one there to call,
I try to forget, but don't at all.
I once left your name to find,
I called it sweet, and good and kind.
But when I found it, it was gone.
You took it back and then moved on.
And so I sit here, cold and blue,
With nothing more for me to do
But sit, with nothing left to say
And throw the roses all away.

# How Do I Break Up with My Boyfriend?

♥

## The heart has eyes which the brain knows nothing of.

Charles Perkhurst

*Dear Kim,*

*I want to break up with my boyfriend, and I don't know how. Please help.*

There are certain things in life that just aren't easy. One of them is breaking up with someone who at one time you loved and possibly still do. Although it is never easy, here are a few guidelines to keep in mind:

- Be as kind about it as you can.
- Be respectful.
- Don't break up with someone in a letter or on a phone message. The only exception to this is if it is a long-distance relationship that has been primarily via letter or e-mail or if you feel that you would be in danger if you broke up.
- Try not to prove your point by listing all the things wrong with him.
- Try not to be defensive. It is very tempting to want to make him wrong and bad and anything else that will alleviate your guilt. Try to remember he will be heartbroken—you can live with a little guilt.
- Even though the line about wanting to still be friends is overused, if you feel that way be sure to tell him. He won't act like he appreciates it, but he will.
- Put yourself in his place. Imagine that he is leaving you and how that would feel. From this perspective figure out what you will say, when you will say it and any other important details. I am by no means suggesting you disregard your own needs. I am only suggesting that you have compassion for him at the same time.
- If there are special circumstances, like he cheated on you or you found out he has been lying to you about something important, this may change the way you handle the situation.
- Don't announce that you are dumping him in front of other people.

- Consider his feelings as much as you can but don't be wishy-washy; in other words, don't give him false hopes.

I also received many letters from guys asking how to break up with their girlfriends. Basically the answer is the same:

- Tell her in person.
- Be respectful of her feelings.
- Be kind.
- Remember this is someone you loved.
- Offer your friendship if you feel that way.
- Don't talk about her to other guys in a mean way. (This goes for the girls, too.) This is one of the saddest and cruelest things that we do. We love someone, we share our feelings with them, our secrets and our hearts and then when we break up we say awful things about them. First of all, if you think about it, it is really insulting yourself, because you loved her or him at one time. But, much more important than that, it is just a really low thing to do. It causes so much hurt, and it isn't necessary.
- Don't discuss things that were personal between the two of you. This is true at all times.

This is for guys and girls:

- When you get into a new relationship don't flaunt it in front of your ex. Remember, things change all the time. You never know who you might be in love with next week or tomorrow. It is always a good idea to behave in a kind and respectful way. What happens if two months from now you fall in love with the girl who saw you act like a real jerk to her friend and now she wants nothing to do with you? *Also,* you want to be respectful because you are going to like yourself more if you are.

# Breaking Up Is Hard to Do

LYNNSEY GARDNER

"So we're really breaking up?" I asked in disbelief, with tears filling my eyes. As my hands became sweaty, my heart pounded against my chest. I felt like bolting out the door and not turning back. How could he do this to me, or more important, to us? I loved Matt, so how could I possibly be losing him?

"We've been together for three-and-a-half years and you know that I have always loved and cared about you. We only have six months before we graduate and I feel that we need to experience new things before we go off to college. I know this is hard for you, but it's hard for me, too. Can't you see that? Some of the happiest times in my life have been with you."

I angrily looked at Matt and screamed, "You're the one ending it!"

"But we can be friends. I don't mean the type that just says 'hi' to each other in the hall, but the type that are always there for one another, in the good times and the bad. Is that too much to ask?"

"Matt, I love you and you have to understand that in the years that we've been together, I never imagined in my wildest dreams that we would break up. You're a part of me, Matt. I find myself happy and carefree when I'm with you. Now, you're asking me to give that up so easily. I don't think I can do that."

"Aren't you listening to me?" Matt asked sharply, holding me by the shoulders and forcing me to look into his deep brown eyes that I often got lost in. I could tell that he was about to break down, too. "I'm happy when I'm with you, too, and I don't plan on giving that up, not *ever!* You're as much a part of me as I am of you. You're my best friend and that's how I always want to keep it. We look out for each other. I didn't want us to have a messy and horrible breakup once high school ends. I didn't want something to come between us to where we can't even talk. That's why I'm ending our couple status, not our friendship."

"Take me home, Matt." I heard my cracking voice say, but I already felt as if I were miles away.

"On one condition," he answered, quickly looking straight at me. He sounded just as tired and worn out by what had happened as I was. "Promise me that you'll think about what I said tonight. Can you do that for me?"

"Yes," I replied, overcome with tears and a wave of emotions. Oh how I wanted to wrap my arms around him again, but I knew that part of us was over—for good.

In the days that followed I drifted around school in a daze. I just didn't feel like being my always smiling, never upset, cheerful self anymore. I wanted to sulk and dwell when my world changed. When friends came up to say how sorry they were for me, I thanked them but insisted they should be sorry for Matt, not me. He was the one that had lost the best thing that ever happened to him.

Often, when we were changing classes, I'd run into Matt in the hall. Instead of speaking, I'd just turn my head in the other direction and toss my blond curly hair confidently over my shoulder. I knew that this was wrong, but I didn't care. He'd hurt me in a way that I couldn't describe, but only express with sheer hatred. When word of what I was saying got back to Matt, he'd simply shrug and murmur, "I'm sorry she feels that way." This only made we feel worse. Every night I'd go home ashamed of what I'd done that day and cry myself to sleep.

One night when I felt as though I couldn't cry anymore, I started reminiscing of the happier times I shared with Matt. Like in seventh grade when we were learning about Shakespeare, and he got up in front of the class, kissed my hand and called me his Juliet. And, on our first date when I was sick and he came over and stayed with me the whole time, telling me I was the most beautiful thing he'd ever seen, even though I looked like Rudolph with my ruby-red nose. And, how he always knew he could fix anything with flowers.

I thought long and hard about what I could do to repair our broken relationship. He meant so much to me that I knew if I shut him out of my life forever, I'd be losing one of the greatest people I'd ever known. I reasoned with myself that a lifelong friendship was much more valuable than hating him for doing what he felt was right. Pushing away my feelings of anger towards Matt, I decided that maybe it was my turn to fix things for the better. The next day I nervously showed up on Matt's doorstep with yellow roses, a sign of friendship.

"When I said, 'I think we should break up,'
I would have liked to have heard at least a sigh of
despair instead of 'Hey, no problem!'"

*Reprinted by permission of Dave Carpenter.*

# Speechless

## KIRA BINDRIM

I wish I could tell you, but not say a word.
My thoughts float out to you, the silent wings of a bird.
My message is simple; I want it to end.
You were so much better as a best friend.
I don't want to hurt you, but there's no other way.
My heart's been telling me what I have to say.
It's not your fault; but yet it has to be.
My reasons are even confusing to me.
They're tangled with detail, too hard to explain.
So please understand and I'll take the blame.
The thoughts in my head must have their say.
I can stand it no longer, the day is today.
I'll tell you the truth, what's been on my mind,
But a good explanation will be hard to find.
You and I together must come to an end,
I now only want you and me to be friends.

# *We Broke Up, and I'm So Depressed*

*Dear Kimberly,*

*My boyfriend and I broke up over two months ago. My friends and my parents kept saying it would get easier with time and I guess it has gotten a little easier, but I am still very sad.*

*I wake up sad, and I go to sleep sad. I don't want to do anything with my friends, and I don't like to be by myself. I am only okay when I am sleeping it seems. Please help me.*

I don't know the details of your sadness, so I want to give two answers to your question.

As I have said many times, it is normal to be sad about the loss of a relationship. Some people take longer to recover than others. Assuming that you are only suffering from this and you are just having a very hard time getting over this relationship, my advice is to be patient and not fight it.

Many times, we fight against our sadness and try to make it go away. By doing that we actually make it stronger. It is best to welcome your sadness, even indulge in it. Of course this can be taken to unhealthy extremes, but if you have only resisted it I suggest you try to "just feel it."

After doing this for a while it should begin to naturally get easier.

The other thing I want to address is the possibility of your being clinically depressed.

Many teens today suffer from depression, and the good news is there are ways to work with it so that you don't have to be depressed. There are medications you can take and there is therapy. Often, both things are recommended.

If you think that what you are going through is more than just a temporary heartache, you want to tell your parents about it and ask them to take you to a doctor to discuss it.

# *Lost*

BECCA WOOLF

You look at me and ask, well, "Why is she so sad?"

She won't tell you that she lost the only love she ever had.

She won't tell you that he loved her and his love was but a lie.

She won't tell you how she waits with desperation in her eye.

She won't tell you that she had him and she threw his love away.

She won't tell you if you ask her, she has nothing left to say.

So don't look at me and ask why she's sitting all alone.

She's trying to forget him, live her life and just move on.

And what she cannot tell you if you ask her why she's sad.

Is she feels like she has lost the only love she ever had.

# Where's My Heart?
# A Ballad

BECCA WOOLF

I lost it not so long ago,
I wait for its return,
The heart in which from in its depths,
My passion used to burn.

And it rumbled up inside me,
Before I even knew,
I let it fly away from me,
And hide inside of you.

I swear to God I will find it,
And love again will I.
To live a life without a heart,
I think I'd rather die.

And when I see you laughing,
I wonder if you know
That though it's been so very long,
I haven't let you go.

And still I lie here crying,
With no heart to call my own,
Cause I lost it with my sanity,
The minute you were gone.

All I ask of you is simple,
To set my spirit free,
To find my old and broken heart,
And give it back to me.

# I Ignored My Friends for Love . . . and Now I Want Them Back

*Dear Kim,*

*My boyfriend and I broke up last week, and I am really upset. I have to get over him and move on, but I have another problem as well. I kind of dumped my friends when I was hanging out with Brian. It wasn't like I was mean to them or anything, I just spent all my time with him and therefore didn't spend any time with them. This weekend I tried to get together with two of my girlfriends, and they blew me off. I know they are mad at me and paying me back. The problem is I really need them right now. What should I do?*

First of all, remember you don't need to feel guilty. Just learn the lesson, forgive yourself and then try to figure out how to make it right again.

Why don't you call them and invite them to come over or go somewhere? (If they won't do that, then write them each a letter.)

If they agree to get together, use the time to share with them what you are going through. Tell them you realize you weren't a great friend and that you let your boyfriend become more important. (We all do it at least once.) Tell them you're sorry, and you certainly never meant to hurt their feelings. Also be sure to tell them what you told me about needing them right now.

I think that this will begin the healing, and you will probably go on to have great fun with them catching up and all. If they are stubborn about forgiving you (and I don't know all the details), then just be patient with them.

It can't be said enough how important friends are and how the saying about them being around long after the guy (or girl) is gone is so true. It sounds like you have learned this lesson and won't make the same mistake again.

# At First

BECCA WOOLF

At first you feel like crying
   and beg God to dry your tears
You sit and reminisce
   of all the good times through the years
You stare at him across the room
   and block that you still care
But you're still in love with the way
   he runs his fingers through his hair
And when you're sick of crying
   but you know you feel the same
You might stop feeling miserable
   and instead hand him the blame
He'll ask you why your friends still vibe
   and you'll turn and walk away
You'll tell him that you hate him
   he'll have nothing left to say
You finally think it's over
   and that this must be the end
But then one day your heart stops
   as he holds his new girlfriend

And you force yourself to realize
   that in time you'll be okay
And the feelings that you felt at first
   will slowly fade away. . . .

# Adios

## LANGLEY WETZEL

Why can't you see what it's doing to you?
And why can't you see that it's killing me, too
What happened to the sweet boy I met?
You told me you loved me, or did you forget?
I thought that I knew you, I thought you were right
But you changed my opinion in one single night
The things that you said, they ripped me apart
And now I am left with this hole in my heart
I know now that You and I will never be We again
I played your game and misery is the prize I win
I thought the pain of losing you would be quite enough
But now I hear you're messing with all kinds of bad stuff
You think getting high will make everything right
But all that you're doing is ruining your life
I watch all you had just slip down the drain
I know I can't help you which drives me insane
I miss all the nights we spent on the phone
The ringing has stopped, I sit here alone
Every day, every night I hope to hear your voice
But I've got to accept that you've made your choice

I hope you know that I'll always care
But next time you need me, I may not be there
You just couldn't love me the way that I was
So now I'm gonna find someone who does

*Ten*

# Starting Over . . . or Here We Go Again

*That's the thing about love and romance—no one can predict where it will take you. Love will fill your heart, break your heart and then heal the heart that's broken.*

Robert Fulghum

# Starting Over

Well, we have been through it all. We have loved, we have kissed, we have won and we have lost. All in the name of love. Poets have compared it to a ride at the carnival, a trip to the heavens and back, and just about anything else you can think of. The one thing everyone agrees on, though, is that no matter how painful, no matter how crazy and no matter how confusing, love is still what makes the world go 'round.

Many of you are reading this chapter and thinking to yourselves, "That's it, I am through with love." We have all felt this way at least once. We have all felt that the pain is too much and it just isn't worth it.

If you feel this way, you will soon change your mind and be ready to love again. In the meantime, use this break to nourish yourself. Use this time to hang out with your friends, try out for the track team or check out those dance classes you've been thinking about. Enjoy your freedom and use it to become more of a whole person. Use it to get stronger and healthier so that when the next one comes along you will be ready.

Most importantly, use this time to heal. Let your

heart mend, and encourage it to stay soft. Many times when love or the lack of it breaks our hearts, we allow our hearts to become brittle and hard. Whatever you do, don't let this happen.

Each new love that you experience will bring you joy and happiness. The amount of love that you can feel, though, depends on the openness of your heart.

# I'm Having a Hard Time Letting Go

*Dear Kim,*

*I have been obsessed over this girl for a long time. I can't help it; I am in love with her. We went out for a while, and it was great. She broke up with me over some little misunderstanding, and she refuses to give me another chance. I feel crazy because she has never even let me explain to her what happened.*

*All my friends tell me to let it go, but I can't. I just want her to at least listen to me, but she won't even talk to me. She won't even be my friend.*

Love is unfair sometimes. Actually it isn't *love* that is unfair, but the circumstances surrounding it are often not what we want them to be or feel they should be.

Your friends are right when they tell you to let it go, and I know this seems like such a hard thing to do. We're not telling you to stop loving her or stop feeling the way you feel. What we are saying is to recognize that there are things that we have no control over. We cannot have control over other people's actions and choices. You can't control what she does or doesn't do.

For your own sanity, it is time to accept this. As you do you will begin to heal, and as you begin to heal you will be open to new and better possibilities.

There *is* a light at the end of this tunnel.

# To Let Go

TIFFANY APPLETON

To let go isn't to forget, not think about, or ignore.
It doesn't leave feelings of anger, jealousy or regret.
Letting go isn't winning and it isn't losing.
It's not about pride and it's not about how you appear,
And it's not obsessing or dwelling on the past.
Letting go isn't blocking memories or thinking sad
    thoughts,
And doesn't leave emptiness, hurt or sadness.
It's not giving in or giving up.
Letting go isn't about loss, and it's not defeat.

To let go is to cherish memories, but to overcome and to
    move on.
It is having an open mind and confidence in the future.
Letting go is accepting,
It is learning and experiencing and growing.
To let go is to be thankful for the experiences that made
    you laugh, made you cry and made you grow.
It's about all that you have, all that you had and all that
    you will soon gain.

Letting go is having the courage to accept change, and the strength to keep moving.

Letting go is growing up.

It is realizing that the heart can sometimes be the most potent remedy.

To let go is to open a door, to clear a path and to set yourself free.

# A New Start

BECCA WOOLF

She lies among a bed of dreams,
In happiness or so it seems.
For it's been long since life began,
And her search goes on for holding hands.
What doesn't kill you makes you strong,
And strength grows wings to fly upon.
She flies on wings so white and pure,
For in her dreams she feels secure.
Lines of songs and verses in rhyme,
Will heal the wounds of bitter time.
No longer will she lie in sadness,
And put on a smile to hide the madness.
Young souls that slip away from tears,
Can strengthen hope through many years.
And with new strength she'll rise above,
Heal her wounds and learn to love.

# My Private Pain

ANONYMOUS

---

When one door closes,
another opens but we often look so
long and so regretfully upon the
closed door that we do not see the
one which has opened for us.

Alexander Graham Bell

---

I am a very private person. It is completely unlike me to even share this, but I have to tell you this story. It is important to me.

Last year marked the end of a very special relationship in my life. The love of my life and I parted ways, and it was the most painful thing I had ever experienced.

The relationship started when I was in third grade. Alan sat across from me in homeroom and four seats behind me in science. We were very cute according to our parents. He would carry my books for me, and I would attempt to make cookies for him after school. We watched too many episodes of the *Wonder Years*. In fact, I was his Winnie, and he was my Kevin.

After years of people telling us this was only puppy love and it would never last, we became official. We went out on a very special date. He took me to a good restaurant and then we went for a walk. He asked if I would be his girlfriend. Oh, it was wonderful. I didn't know I could feel so good and so happy and even more in love than I was before. He felt the same way.

As to not bore you completely, I will skip ahead to high school, junior year. . . . We are still together. The longest-lasting couple was a title we wore proudly, and we were heading for our ten-year anniversary. I didn't know what life was like without him.

To this day, Alan says he wasn't looking to fall in love with someone else, it just happened. I always have trouble with this because I wonder how do these things just happen. You just happened to find yourself together with her in the backseat of your car? Whatever.

When he first told me I thought I would be angry and make him promise to never do anything like this again. Then we would kiss, make up and recover; after all we were Alan and Beth. He didn't give me that option, though. He actually told me straight up that he was in love with this other girl—that we were over, finished, and my only option was to be his friend. Somehow this did not make me feel even a little bit better about the situation.

It is still hard for me to talk about the next part because it was so hard. All the words like pain and misery just scratch the surface of what I was feeling. My parents and my close friends became concerned.

"Maybe you should talk to someone," my mother would say in a really gentle tone.

My girlfriends tried to fix me up, talk bad about Alan, not talk about Alan and get me to go out with them on the weekends. I could tell everyone was worried about me, but I remained in a daze.

Two months after Alan left me, I attempted suicide. I overdosed on pills, all different kinds that I had been collecting. It was awful. As soon as I swallowed the last bunch, I absolutely freaked out. I started screaming for my mom, and she didn't hear me. I was so afraid I would die before I could fix this horrible mistake I had made. Finally, I got the nerve to call 911, and this is what saved my life. Once I was stable they told me I had to spend a week in the psychiatric ward of the hospital. Three days was the law and the extra four was what they determined I would need to get back on track. These were their words, not mine.

Now I cried for a different reason. Alan was a distant memory, and I realized he had little to do with the pain I had been feeling. I was crying for myself, for the love I wanted so badly to feel, for the times that I was too embarrassed to say I want a hug, I need some love. They gave me a label: codependent. Basically it means I take care of others before myself. This was the pain I was feeling. I needed to learn to take care of myself. I needed to learn to love myself. Alan had been doing the job for way too long. We were just kids, and we had become everything to each other.

I really don't want to preach because I hate it when people do it to me. But please let me say one thing. When I swallowed those pills, I was so frightened. I have never known fear like this. I wanted to live with every cell in my body, and I had almost taken my own life away. Please don't do what I did, no matter what.

I am a very private person, but I had to tell this story, because I care.

# What If I Get Hurt Again?

Life shrinks or expands according
to one's courage.

Anaïs Nin

*Dear Kim,*

*When Jeremy and I broke up I swore that was it for me. The other night I went over to my friend's house and there were some people there hanging out.*

*There was this guy, Dave, who I have met before but never thought much about. Well, we started talking and I was having a real nice time with him, and when I got ready to go, he kissed me. Then he asked if he could walk me home, which I thought was really sweet. So here I am, in love again. Problem is, I'm scared. I got so hurt last time, and I don't think I could take it again.*

The first breakup is the worst, in my opinion. You have never experienced that kind of rejection before, so it hits you like a ton of bricks. After you have gone through it once, it gets a little bit easier. Actually, not easier, it's just that you know you will recover. The first time it happens, you don't think you ever will. You have recovered, right? Remember this.

Pain actually helps us to grow, makes us stronger and often makes us better people. It has been compared to the process of coal being turned into diamonds, or the irritant in an oyster that makes the pearl. We don't want to become so afraid of pain that we don't allow ourselves to feel and to love.

It sounds like you have chosen life over fear, so let me congratulate you.

Enjoy the love that comes your way and know that the pain is part of the deal. Remember that you have the ability to heal and the capacity to endure some pain. Life is scary when we don't know what to expect. You have already experienced the worst that can happen with love: heartbreak. Trust the wisdom in your heart that knows that you are ready for love again.

# Chasm of the Heart

RACHEL MILLER

Pebble of old feelings
and budding flowers of new
line the bottom of the chasm
where emotions run through
like a fast and violent tide
which gives love life
and cuts down sense and reason
like a sharp-bladed knife.

Though these tides sometimes lessen
and the chasm runs dry
the bitter roots begin to flourish
and the beauty starts to die
the tide will always return
bringing beauty again with full force
replenishing blossoms and new hopes
as it swiftly runs its course.

# Footprints in My Heart

LAUREN OLSZEWSKI

Chris and I spent our junior year of high school together. He changed my life in more ways than I could ever put into words. He taught me how to love, and that there really was such a thing as a soul mate. He held my hand through some of the most difficult times of my life, and was always there with a reassuring "I love you" when that was all I needed. He told me that we were meant for each other, and we'd be together forever. And after the seven months that we were together, that's what I believed.

This is why our breakup came as such a shock to me. He called me one night, just as I was walking in the door from work. I said "Hi" in my usual cheery voice, but the expression on the other end wasn't the happy reply I usually got. He simply told me that he felt it was time that we see other people. He said that he was sorry, and he still wanted to be best friends. He said that he hoped I'd understand. But everything he said came without emotion, as if he were reading it off of a paper.

But the thing that I didn't understand the most wasn't

the fact that he didn't want to be with me anymore, or how he could walk away from the past seven months like nothing had ever happened. It was how he expected me to remain his best friend. Best friends have relationships so strong that nothing could ever come between them. They have the kind of friendship that is built on honesty, trust and love. And in the past five minutes, Chris had managed to take all of these from me.

The next day in school was harder for me than I thought it would be. Our lockers were right next to each other, and he said that he wasn't going to move his, because he felt it would bring us farther apart. This put me in a very uncomfortable position between each class period, but I was trying to make myself okay with us not being together, so I didn't say anything. Instead, I tried to look at him and see him as my friend, before our friendship grew into a love. I tried to look at him and forget the past seven months, because he made it look so easy. But all I saw was all the love and time I'd given to him, and all the pain I received.

The next several months were the hardest for me as Chris tried to stay a part of my life. I wasn't a strong enough person to talk to him on the phone and see him every day with all the hurt I was feeling inside. I still felt like half of a person without him. Two weeks later, the school year ended. This is when I was able to begin the process of healing. It took a lot of time, and I knew that I needed to be patient. I had more time to myself because the summer had arrived, and I spent a lot of time thinking about the past. Things still weren't clear in my mind, but I began to accept them. Slowly the pain lessened, and I was able to laugh and smile again. I was able to go out with my best friends for the night without him crossing my mind.

There are times when I wish we were still together, because of all the wonderful memories we had together. But then again there are times when it hurts too much to even consider the friendship. I know I feel a lot better about myself now, but I'm still healing. It will take time, but I know now that I will be okay.

# I Just Moved, and It's Hard to Start Over

Life is either a daring adventure
or nothing. To keep our faces toward
change and behave like free spirits
in the presence of fate is
strength undefeatable.

Helen Keller

*Dear Kim,*

*We just moved from Indiana to California. I am in the tenth grade. When I first found out that we had to leave Fort Wayne, I was a mess. I would be leaving all my friends and even worse, my boyfriend. I was, according to my mother, a wreck. I have been in Los Angeles for just over a month now, and although it has been hard, it hasn't been near as bad as I thought. In fact, it got a lot better when I* met Scotty. *Before I come off sounding like I just forgo* *about my old boyfriend, let me explain. We decided when* *found out I was moving to break up before I left. It was bet-* *ter this way because when we got real upset we could stil* *see each other and hold each other. We knew if we waited* *till I moved, we wouldn't be able to do that.*

*We ended our relationship as friends, and I wil* *always love him. He doesn't expect me to sit around and* *wait for him though. I guess we are too realistic for that*

*Scotty is a real nice guy, real cute, too. We have gone* *out twice, and I like him very much. I am pretty sure he* *likes me, too. I'm just a little nervous because everything* *is so new. I am in a new city, going to a new school, try-* *ing to make new friends and now seeing a new guy. My* *friends say he is nice and they like him, it is just that* *because I have been here for such a short time, I feel like* *I don't really know what I am getting myself into.*

When I was growing up, I had to move seven times. I moved in the middle of ninth grade, and I had to leave my boyfriend behind. I didn't hate my new life; it was just that I missed that feeling of belonging that takes time to acquire. I made some big mistakes. I got involved with some people who I didn't know well enough and had to learn some tough lessons very quickly.

However, you sound like you are already in better shape than I was.

Since I don't know all the details of your situation, let's just say you can't be too careful. Assuming you feel safe with your new friends, and with Scotty, take things slow and get to know everyone.

If you have bigger questions that you were afraid to ask, be sure to talk to someone about it. Teachers are always available to talk, and they know everyone pretty well.

You sound like a very mature girl, and I believe you will be fine. Remember that change is always hard and making a new life in a new city is one of the most stressful things you will ever have to do. Don't underestimate it, and be good to yourself. The biggest mistake we can make is belittling our own process. We have to trust our instincts, and we have to be understanding of *ourselves* when we are going through something that is difficult.

# I'm Having Fun on My Own!

♥

I no longer have the fear of being alone. It's cool to find out that you don't need a boyfriend to be happy.

Drew Barrymore

*Dear Kim,*

*From the time I was in seventh grade until about six months ago, I always had a boyfriend. I would go from one to the other. In fact, I usually waited until I had a new boyfriend before I broke up with the old one. Pretty lame, huh?*

*For the last six months, though, I have been on my own and I have actually had a great time. I have no intention of remaining single for the rest of my life, but I am having a blast right now being alone.*

*On the weekend I don't have to wait to see what "he" is doing before I make plans. I don't sit around and wait for "him" to call, and I am not worrying all the time whether or not "he" is mad, jealous, upset or whatever.*

*I just wanted to tell other girls my age that you don't have to have a boyfriend to be happy. Now when I do fall in love, I think it is going to be special because it isn't out of some big need to have a boyfriend.*

What a great message.
Thanks for sharing it.

# Who Needs a Boyfriend Anyway?

SHELBY WOODARD

So who needs a boyfriend anyway?
That's the conclusion I came to today.
It's not so bad being just one
Actually, it can be quite fun.
Hanging out at the mall all day,
Appreciating your friends in a new special way.
Never having to worry about him,
Whether he be Aaron, Chris, Michael or Jim.
Which movie to rent on Saturday night
Is no longer an issue that ends in a fight.
Going where you want, seeing who you please
Even though you miss having someone to tease.
Three-hour phone calls about nothing at all
Become three-hour shopping trips with
Mom at the mall.
You see more of your little sister now, too,
Being surprised at how much she grew.

But please, I ask, don't shed a tear.
I know that your heart must be filled with fear.
Being alone can be rough at first
But it only gets better, it doesn't get worse.
Soon enough you'll love once more
But for now, it's yourself you should adore.
Look at every day with a new brighter light
And I'm sure, like me, in time you'll be all right.

# I'm Becoming Obsessed Again!

*Dear Kim,*

*Is it possible to be happy and sad and scared all at the same time?*

*Last year I went through a horrible breakup, and I swore I would never fall in love again. Of course I knew I wasn't being realistic, but since then I have managed to keep my distance from guys. I have dated, but I haven't let myself do those things like sit by the phone waiting for his call or staying home in hopes he will stop by. It has been great to be free from all that, and I believed it was because I had learned my lesson and grown up.*

*Well, three weeks ago I met this guy. I knew him from school but not personally. He is a senior, and I am a junior. My friends don't hang out with his. Anyway, we met at a party and instantly hit it off. We talked to each other the entire time, and he said he would call me the next day.*

*Saturday I woke up so excited. My girlfriends called around 11:00 A.M. to say they were going to pick me up at noon to go to this dance recital that some of our other friends were performing in. After that we would all probably go see a movie or something. I panicked. If I went I might miss his call, but if I didn't then what's up with that? I made up some lame excuse about my parents, and I know my friends didn't believe me. I felt so crappy all day because I hated myself for what I had done.*

*He called but not until 5:00, which meant I would have been home in time to talk to him. To make matters worse, he said, "Sorry I didn't call sooner, but I had plans with my friends and we just got back."*

*We have been hanging out for a couple of weeks now, and it is really nice. But I am still doing the same thing by waiting for him and not making other plans. I try to stop, but whenever I have to make a choice I can't risk not seeing him.*

*I need help. My friends are disappointed in me, and I am more than disappointed in myself.*

This hits really close to home.

When I was (much) younger I fell in love with a guy; we will call him Rob. I hadn't ever felt this way about a guy in my life, and he felt the same way. Even today I remember how incredible it was to love someone like that. As the relationship developed, I fell more in love with him. I also became more insecure. As much as I loved him and wanted to be with him, I also was afraid of losing him. It would not be bearable. He was an independent guy and liked hanging out with his friends on the weekends, going to games and so on. He was always straight with me, but he would say things like, "Maybe I'll stop by after the game," or "If I'm not too tired I'll call you when I get home." That was all it took for me to sit around and wait for him. The more I behaved this way, the more my own confidence decreased. I began to feel desperate. Let's face it: I was.

I would justify it by saying that I loved being with him and it was worth it to give up other plans just for the possibility of seeing him.

He began to notice that I was *always* home and *always* available, and he said things like, "Kim, I don't want you to sit around and wait for me. Go out and have fun, I'll see you tomorrow." *Ouch.* He even stopped saying he might stop by because he knew I would sit around and wait for him.

My self-esteem continued on a downward spiral, and he became more and more withdrawn. I knew he loved me, but the way I was handling myself was beginning to scare him and put him off. The strange thing is I knew this, but I still couldn't change my behavior. It was like I was addicted to him.

After being together for almost three years he began to talk about taking a break. At this time if I could have been strong and if I could have regained my *self* there would have been a possibility for us to continue. But I couldn't. To this day I am certain that he loved me very much. What he didn't love was a me with no self-respect or ability to maintain my identity. In essence there was no me left to love and that was the problem.

So in answer to your question, I say fake it till you make it. Translation: Go out with your girlfriends even if it is against every cell in your body to do so. Make plans, have a life and do what is necessary to maintain your self-respect. This is the only option if what you want is a healthy relationship—with him and with yourself.

Jenny showed no special athletic aptitude in school,
but broke numerous speed records
answering the telephone.

*Reprinted by permission of Randy Glasbergen.*

# In Closing

Well, we could go on and on from here, but all good things must come to an end.

Putting this book together has been one of the most exciting and fun-filled things I have ever done. It has also been heartwrenching and heartbreaking at times because of the suffering involved in something so absolutely wonderful as love.

I hope that while reading this book you have been able to feel the love and compassion I have for each and every one of you. Going through adolescence and having to make sense out of all of it by yourself is something that should never be expected, and yet very few people are willing to treat it as seriously as it deserves. Once again it is my deepest hope that I have treated it with the respect and sincerity that it and you deserve.

Please write to me and tell me what you think, what you liked and what you learned.

Also, remember, the next book I am doing in the *Teen Love* series is *On Friendship*, and it promises to be as good and as helpful as this one has been. Please send us poetry and questions and stories about friendship and the challenges it presents.

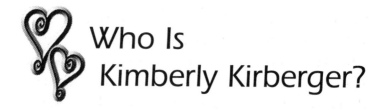

# Who Is Kimberly Kirberger?

Kimberly Kirberger is the president and founder of I.A.M. for Teens (Inspiration and Motivation for Teens), a corporation formed exclusively to work *for* teens. Her goal is to see teens represented in a more positive light; her strong belief is that teens deserve better and more positive treatment.

She spends her time reading the thousands of letters and stories sent to her by teen readers and traveling around the country speaking to high school students and parents of teens. She has appeared as a teen expert on many television and radio shows, including *Geraldo,* MSNBC and the *Terry Bradshaw Show.*

Kimberly is the coauthor of the bestselling *Chicken Soup for the Teenage Soul* and *New York Times* #1 bestseller *Chicken Soup for the Teenage Soul II,* as well as *Chicken Soup for the Teenage Soul Journal.* She is also the coauthor of *Chicken Soup for the College Soul,* and the forthcoming *Chicken Soup for the Parent's Soul, Chicken Soup for the Teenage Soul III* and *Chicken Soup for the Teenage Soul Letters.* In addition, she is the author of the *Teen Love* series, which includes this book and four forthcoming titles, three of them workbooks.

Kimberly started the Teen Letter Project with Jack Canfield, Mark Victor Hansen and Health Communications, Inc. The Project is responsible for answering the heartfelt letters received from teenagers and also reaching out to teens in trouble and encouraging them to seek professional help.

To book Kimberly for a speaking engagement or for further information on any of her projects, please contact:

### I.A.M. for Teens, Inc.

P.O. Box 936 • Pacific Palisades, CA 90272

phone: 310-573-3655 • fax: 310-573-3657

e-mail for stories: *stories@teenagechickensoup.com*

e-mail for letters: *letters@teenagechickensoup.com*

e-mail for questions and/or submissions

for the *Teen Love* series: *kim@teenlove.com*

Web site: *www.teenagechickensoup.com*

# Contributors

**Tiffany Appleton** is eighteen years old and a freshman at the University of Arizona. She hopes to continue writing and has received her ambition for writing from her father. She can be reached by e-mail at *tiffany@u.arizona.edu*.

**Julian Arizona** is a sophomore in high school. She is sixteen years old and has an older brother, Alex, who is twenty. She loves animals and horseback riding. She plans to become a veterinarian and publish poetry on the side. In her free time, she loves to hang out with friends. She also loves singing and swimming. Her poem is dedicated to all crushes, and to her family and friends.

**Amanda Bailey** is seventeen years old and involved in volleyball, show-choir, youth ministry, and leading younger girls in Bible study. Her heart lies in her music and writing, which she uses not only to express herself, but also to share her faith in the Lord—the most important part of her life. She can be reached by e-mail at *AGBprincess@aol.com*.

**Kara L. Bailey** is nineteen years old and currently a student at Salisbury State University. She is majoring in respiratory therapy but hopes to someday become a paramedic. She is also a member of the Mardela Springs Volunteer Fire department as a firefighter and emergency medical technician. She enjoys listening to music, reading and watching her nephew, Zackery and niece, Brittany.

**Rachel Bentley** is the daughter of foster-care providers. She has had plenty of opportunity to glean insights from seeing into the hearts of people, and gain an understanding of the reasons they often behave as they do. She loves her family and what they do, and wouldn't exchange them for the world.

**Kira Bindrim** has been writing stories, poems and essays since elementary school. She has won several writing awards, is senior editor of her school's literary magazine and sincerely hopes to continue writing through the years. She can be reached by e-mail at *kirasue13@hotmail.com.*

**Katie Brennan** is a junior in high school. She wrote her story, "The Perfect Guy?" in February 1998. Katie is the opinion editor of her award-winning school newspaper, the *Prosepector.* She feels honored to share her first published story with *Teen Love,* and hopes to contribute more efforts in the future. Katie would like to thank her family and friends for their support and inspiration.

**Dave Carpenter** has been a full-time cartoonist since 1981. His cartoons have appeared in a variety of publications including *Barron's, Harvard Business Review,* the *Wall Street Journal,* the *Saturday Evening Post, Better Homes and Gardens, Good Housekeeping, Forbes, Woman's World,* as well as numerous other publications. Dave can be reached at P.O. Box 520, Emmetsburg, IA 50536.

**Ron Cheng** is a student at Rutgers University, majoring in marketing with a minor in psychology. Writing is one of his many hobbies, along with Web-page design and graphics. Ron can be reached by e-mail at *ron@ricebowl.net.*

**Sara Corbin** is a high-school student involved in FHA, junior beta, speech/drama, student council, volleyball and choir. She is also class president. Her hobbies include horseback riding, poetry, songwriting and sports. Her personal hero is her grandmother.

**Allison Forster** is a fourteen-year-old eighth-grader who enjoys playing soccer, running track, dancing and singing. She also is involved with the student council. When she is older, she would like to become an English teacher because she loves helping others. She dedicates *The Kiss* to Ryan, her first love and her angel. She hopes they stay together forever!

**Lynnsey Gardner** is a high-school student. Her interests include softball, working with small children, learning the Spanish language, mock trial and writing. Her real passion lies in drama and she hopes to one day become an actress. She thanks her eighth-grade English teachers, Susan Demos and Ann Marie Nault, for inspiring her to write. She also thanks her family and friends for their support through the years.

**Kelly Garnett** is a twenty-one-year-old college student studying elementary education and language arts. She would like to thank her family and friends who have taught her what it means to love and how lucky she is to be loved in return.

**Randy Glasbergen** is one of America's most widely and frequently published humorous artists. More than twenty-five thousand of his cartoons and illustrations have been published by *Campus Life, Funny Times, Glamour, Cosmopolitan* and many others. His daily comic panel, *The Better Half,* is syndicated worldwide by King Features Syndicate. For more of Randy's cartoons, please visit his Web site: *www.glasbergen.com.*

**Jennifer Hadra** is a high-school junior. She enjoys cheerleading, softball, and spending time with her friends and family. Jennifer has been penning her thoughts and feelings since first grade. She plans to pursue a career in broadcast journalism. She is grateful to God for his unfailing love, to John for the inspiration behind the poem, and to her parents for believing in her 100 percent. Jennifer can be reached at *JLynn104@AOL.com.*

**Briana Halpin** has been described in a variety of ways—goofy, brilliant, misanthropic, compassionate, artistic, intuitive, hilarious, romantic, amazing, sensitive, cynical, intense, awkward—but the adjective most often used in the same sentence as her name is *insane.* She says: "Insanity is the rational response to an irrational world, *n'est ce-pas?*" She can be reached by e-mail at *stargazer176@juno.com.*

**Chelsea Hellings** is a sixteen-year-old eleventh-grader. She has an older brother, Rory, and an older sister, Lindsay. Chelsea enjoys volleyball, basketball, hockey, drama and public speaking. She is the director of the junior-high drama club and writes for the school newspaper, the *Nordic News.* Chelsea plans to pursue a career in medicine. She can be reached by e-mail at *chellings@hotmail.com.*

**Samantha Joseph** is a junior in high school. An honor student, she enjoys acting, writing and playing the drums. Samantha would like to thank all of the wonderful and incredible people in her life. She dedicates this story to them.

**Erin Kelly** is a twenty-one-year-old senior at Seton Hall University, studying English education and psychology. She is the secretary and treasurer of her school's student activities board and plans many events. "With Honor" is her first published work. She would like to thank her family, friends, Mrs. Carolan and Mrs. Korner for believing in her and encouraging her to seek publication of her poems.

**Kristine Lee** is a secondary-school student from CHIJ St. Nicholas Girl's School in Singapore. One of her main hobbies is writing. This is her first published piece of work, and she aspires to pursue a career in journalism. She can be reached at *kristine08@hotmail.com*.

**Kim Llerena** is having a blast being fifteen years old and a freshman in high school. She has written a column for her town newspaper for three years. Her hobbies include performing in high-school plays, swimming on two teams, and photography and the visual arts. She aspires to become a photojournalist.

**Rachel Miller** perceives herself as friendly, open-minded and understanding. Among other things, she enjoys playing piano, reading, writing, drawing, painting and spending time with her family and friends. Although she enjoys all competitive sports, badminton is her favorite and she is on her school's team. She loves *Chicken Soup* books!

**Sara Nachtman** graduated from Walhert High School this year and plans to attend the University of Northern Iowa in the fall as a biology major and a double minor in French and English. She also plans to swim competitively for UNI. The response to her material in *Chicken Soup for the Teenage Soul II* so impressed her that it encouraged her to keep writing. She enjoys questions and comments, and can be reached by e-mail at *swmnachts@aol.com*.

**Kent Nerburn** is an author, sculptor and educator who has been deeply involved in Native American issues and education. He has served as project director for two books of oral history entitled, *To Walk the Red Road* and *We Choose to Remember*. He has also edited three highly acclaimed books on Native American subjects. Kent won the Minnesota Award for his book, *Neither Wolf nor Dog: On Forgotten Roads in 1995*. Kent holds a Ph.D. in theology and art and lives with his family in Bemidju, Minnesota.

**Brandy Nicholas** is nineteen years old. In 1998, she graduated from Peninsula High School, where she learned to use her writing skills from her English teacher, Judy Cromitt. She has been writing since she was five years old and published her first book when she was in first grade. She enjoys music and being with her animals and the people she loves most. Her inspirations are her mom and dad, Mrs. Cromitt and her friends. She can be reached by e-mail at *evertight@hotmail.com*.

**Olivia Odom** is fifteen years old and a ninth-grader. She enjoys writing poetry and photography. Her favorite writer is William Shakespeare and her favorite photographer is Mangelson. Her favorite class is English because she has a lot of writing assignments. She says that nothing in particular inspired her to write, but she gets her best ideas from her family and friends. She spends most of her time hanging out with her friends and talking to her sister.

**Lauren Olszewski** is a seventeen-year-old high-school senior. She will be attending the University of Rhode Island in the fall of 1999, where she will pursue a career in nursing. She loves to dance and has been taking classes for ten years. Lauren would like to thank her best friend, Christina Olszewski, for everything. She can be reached by e-mail at *Dance2157@juno.com*.

**Amy Ortega** is sixteen years old. She plays sports and loves to read and write. She lives with her parents and two younger sisters. The stories she wrote in the past came from her imagination. This year, she decided to write something real about her life, and *Teen Love* provided the perfect opportunity. Someday, she hopes to become a real author.

**Tammy Osborne** is a high-school sophomore. After high school, she plans to major in choral music education at NAU. It is her dream to conduct her own junior-high-school choir. In her free time she enjoys writing short stories and poetry.

**Miriam Perez** is fourteen years old and a freshman in high school. Her parents are originally from Havana, Cuba and they migrated to the United States in the 1960s. She can be reached by e-mail at *perefamily@mindspring.com*.

**Harley Schwadron** is based in Ann Arbor, Michigan. A professional cartoonist for more than twenty years, his cartoons appear in *Barron's*, the *Wall Street Journal, Harvard Business Review, National Law Journal, Medical Economics* and other periodicals. Previously, he worked as a newspaper reporter and public-relations editor, but he always aspired to be a cartoonist. He can be reached at P.O. Box 1347, Ann Arbor, MI 48106.

**Rebecca Scida** is nineteen years old. She attends the Indiana

University of Pennsylvania, where she is an English major, with a minor in journalism. She loves reading and writing, and aspires to be a well-respected author.

**Tiffany Storm,** age nineteen, is currently studying English at the University of Wisconsin at Madison. Hoping to become an English professor, Tiffany enjoys every aspect of literature, including the communication, as well as the sentiment, that it provides. She would like to thank Mummie, Daddy, Justin, Jonathan and Sam for teaching her how to learn from her mistakes and appreciate every moment given to her. She can be reached at *tjstorm@students.wisc.edu.*

**Meredee Switzer** is currently working full-time and plans to begin her freshman year of college this fall, hoping to pursue a business degree. This is her first published work. Her interests include biking, swimming, cooking, art and playing the piano. She can be reached at *Meredee_Switzer@Hotmail.com.*

**Jane Watkins** is a true renaissance woman. She is a multimedia artist, deep-tissue bodywork practitioner, dancer, poet and world-class athlete specializing in Hawaiian outrigger canoeing. She lives and works in Santa Monica, California.

**Langley Wetzel** wrote this poem, her first published work, at age fifteen. She is presently a student at the University of Kentucky. In addition to writing, Langley enjoys photography, scrapbooking, collecting quotes, softball, and spending time with her family and friends. She can be reached at *Langaroo@aol.com.*

**Shelby Woodard** is a seventeen-year-old, home-schooled senior, who lives with her parents and two lizards, Blitz and Benz. She thanks her mother and five older sisters who, through their own experiences, have taught her: "Who needs a boyfriend anyway." She dedicates her story to them and says, now it's time to pass it on to Kayonna and Alana!

**Becca Woolf** is currently a freshman at Loyola Marymount University in Los Angeles majoring in TV/film production. She has been published in *Chicken Soup for the Teenage Soul II* and is currently working on her own memoir, entitled *Broken Mirrors.* She has appeared as a guest on MSNBC and has produced segments for XETV FOX's *Freshpoint.* Becca also gives talks to elementary- and junior-high-school students about the influence and importance of writing. She wishes to thank

Kimberly Kirberger for her support and inspiration, and for giving her the opportunity to inspire others. She can be reached by e-mail at *rebeccawoolf@hotmail.com.*

**Nina Yocco** graduated from high school in June 1999. She will attend Penn State in the fall and plans to study communications. In her free time she enjoys reading, writing short stories, and spending time with her family, friends and yellow Lab, Madison.

# Permissions

**Permissions** *(continued from page iv)*

*The Perfect Guy?* Reprinted by permission of Katie Brennan. ©1999 Katie Brennan.

*You Tell Me.* Reprinted by permission of Kim Llerena. ©1999 Kim Llerena.

*Stone by Stone.* Reprinted by permission of Rachel Bentley. ©1999 Rachel Bentley.

*The Pit of Love.* Reprinted by permission of Jennifer Hadra. ©1999 Jennifer Hadra.

*My Special Someone.* Reprinted by permission of Kristine Lee. ©1999 Kristine Lee.

*The "L" Word.* Reprinted by permission of Amanda Bailey. ©1999 Amanda Bailey.

*Sister.* Reprinted by permission of Becca Woolf. ©1999 Becca Woolf.

*Alone.* Reprinted by permission of Becca Woolf. ©1999 Becca Woolf.

*First Time.* Reprinted by permission of Jane Watkins. ©1999 Jane Watkins.

*First Kiss.* Reprinted by permission of Ron Cheng. ©1999 Ron Cheng.

*The Kiss.* Reprinted by permission of Allison Forster. ©1999 Allison Forster.

*Love Is Sweet.* Reprinted by permission of Tiffany Storm. ©1999 Tiffany Storm.

*The Boy Next Door.* Reprinted by permission of Becca Woolf. ©1999 Becca Woolf.

*Illusion.* Reprinted by permission of Julian Arizona. ©1999 Julian Arizona.

*Sweet Dreams.* Reprinted by permission of Kelly Garnett. ©1999 Kelly Garnett.

*Someone Special.* Reprinted by permission of Olivia Odom. ©1999 Olivia Odom.

*My Best Friend.* Reprinted by permission of Samantha Joseph. ©1999 Samantha Joseph.

# Also from Kim Kirberger
## Bestselling Chicken Soup for Teens

Collect all three of the *Chicken Soup for the Teenage Soul*
volumes. Bestselling stories from teens on learning to embrace life,
becoming the person you can be, being happy with who you are
and loving yourself.

Code #4630 • $12.95

Code #6161 • $12.95

Code #6374 • $12.95